A
THEOLOGICO-POLITICAL
TREATISE

PART IV
CHAPTERS XVI TO XX

A
THEOLOGICO-POLITICAL
TREATISE

PART IV
CHAPTERS XVI TO XX

By
BENEDICT DE SPINOZA

Also known as
BARUCH SPINOZA

ARC
MANOR
ROCKVILLE, MARYLAND
2008

ISBN: 978-1-60450-216-9

Published by Arc Manor
P. O. Box 10339
Rockville, MD 20849-0339
www.ArcManor.com
Printed in the United States of America/United Kingdom

CONTENTS

CHAPTER XVI

Of the Foundations of A State; Of the Natural and Civil Rights of Individuals; And of the Rights of the Sovereign Power.

HITHERTO our care has been to separate philosophy from theology, and to show the freedom of thought which such separation insures to both. It is now time to determine the limits to which such freedom of thought and discussion may extend itself in the ideal state. For the due consideration of this question we must examine the foundations of a State, first turning our attention to the natural rights of individuals, and afterwards to religion and the state as a whole.

By the right and ordinance of nature, I merely mean those natural laws wherewith we conceive every individual to be conditioned by nature, so as to live and act in a given way. For instance, fishes are naturally conditioned for swimming, and the greater for devouring the less; therefore fishes enjoy the water, and the greater devour the less by sovereign natural right. For it is certain that nature, taken in the abstract, has sovereign right to do anything, she can; in other words, her right is coextensive with her power. The power of nature is the power of God, which has sovereign right over all things; and, inasmuch as the power of nature is simply the aggregate of the powers of all her individual components, it follows that every, individual has sovereign right to do all that he can; in other words, the rights of an individual extend to the utmost limits of his power as it has been conditioned. Now it is the sovereign law and right of nature that each individual should endeavour to preserve itself as it is, without regard to anything

7

but itself ; therefore this sovereign law and right belongs to every individual, namely, to exist and act according to its natural conditions. We do not here acknowledge any difference between mankind and other individual natural entities, nor between men endowed with reason and those to whom reason is unknown; nor between fools, madmen, and sane men. Whatsoever an individual does by the laws of its nature it has a sovereign right to do, inasmuch as it acts as it was conditioned by nature, and cannot act otherwise. Wherefore among men, so long as they are considered as living under the sway of nature, he who does not yet know reason, or who has not yet acquired the habit of virtue, acts solely according to the laws of his desire with as sovereign a right as he who orders his life entirely by the laws of reason.

That is, as the wise man has sovereign right to do all that reason dictates, or to live according to the laws of reason, so also the ignorant and foolish man has sovereign right to do all that desire dictates, or to live according to the laws of desire. This is identical with the teaching of Paul, who acknowledges that previous to the law—that is, so long as men are considered of as living under the sway of nature, there is no sin.

The natural right of the individual man is thus determined, not by sound reason, but by desire and power. All are not naturally conditioned so as to act according to the laws and rules of reason; nay, on the contrary, all men are born ignorant, and before they can learn the right way of life and acquire the habit of virtue, the greater part of their life, even if they have been well brought up, has passed away. Nevertheless, they are in the meanwhile bound to live and preserve themselves as far as they can by the unaided impulses of desire. Nature has given them no other guide, and has denied them the present power of living according to sound reason; so that they are no more bound to live by the dictates of an enlightened mind, than a cat is bound to live by the laws of the nature of a lion.

Whatsoever, therefore, an individual (considered as under the sway of nature) thinks useful for himself, whether led by sound reason or impelled by the passions, that he has a sovereign right to seek and to take for himself as he best can, whether by force, cunning, entreaty, or any other means; consequently he may regard as an enemy anyone who hinders the accomplishment of his purpose.

It follows from what we have said that the right and ordinance of nature, under which all men are born, and under which they mostly live, only prohibits such things as no one desires, and no one can attain: it does not forbid strife, nor hatred, nor anger, nor deceit, nor, indeed, any of the means suggested by desire.

This we need not wonder at, for nature is not bounded by the laws of human reason, which aims only at man's true benefit and preservation; her limits are infinitely wider, and have reference to the eternal order of nature, wherein man is but a speck; it is by the necessity of this alone that all individuals are conditioned for living and acting in a particular way. If anything, therefore, in nature seems to us ridiculous, absurd, or evil, it is because we only know in part, and are almost entirely ignorant of the order and interdependence of nature as a whole, and also because we want everything to be arranged according to the dictates of our human reason; in reality that which reason considers evil, is not evil in respect to the order and laws of nature as a whole, but only in respect to the laws of our reason.

Nevertheless, no one can doubt that it is much better for us to live according to the laws and assured dictates of reason, for, as we said, they have men's true good for their object. Moreover, everyone wishes to live as far as possible securely beyond the reach of fear, and this would be quite impossible so long as everyone did everything he liked, and reason's claim was lowered to a par with those of hatred and anger; there is no one who is not ill at ease in the midst of enmity, hatred, anger, and deceit, and who does not seek to avoid them as much as he can. When we reflect that men without mutual help, or the aid of reason, must needs live most miserably, as we clearly proved in Chap. v., we shall plainly see that men must necessarily come to an agreement to live together as securely and well as possible if they are to enjoy as a whole the rights which naturally belong to them as individuals, and their life should be no more conditioned by the force and desire of individuals, but by the power and will of the whole body. This end they will be unable to attain if desire be their only guide (for by the laws of desire each man is drawn in a different direction); they must, therefore, most firmly decree and establish that they will be guided in everything by reason (which nobody will dare openly to repudiate lest he should be taken for a madman), and will restrain any desire which is injurious to a man's fellows, that they will do to all as they would be done by, and that they will defend their neighbour's rights as their own.

How such a compact as this should be entered into, how ratified and established, we will now inquire.

Now it is a universal law of human nature that no one ever neglects anything which he judges to be good, except with the hope of gaining a greater good, or from the fear of a greater evil; nor does anyone endure an evil except for the sake of avoiding a greater evil, or gaining a greater good. That is, everyone will, of two goods, choose that which he thinks the greatest; and, of two evils, that which he thinks the least. I say advisedly that which he thinks the greatest or the least, for it does not necessarily follow that he judges right. This law is so deeply implanted in the human mind that it ought to be counted among eternal truths and axioms.

As a necessary consequence of the principle just enunciated, no one can honestly promise to forego the right which he has over all things,[1] and in general no one will abide by his promises, unless under the fear of a greater evil, or the hope of a greater good. An example will make the matter clearer. Suppose that a robber forces me to promise that I will give him my goods at his will and pleasure. It is plain (inasmuch as my natural right is, as I have shown, co-extensive with my power) that if I can free myself from this robber by stratagem, by assenting to his demands, I have the natural right to do so, and

---

1   See Endnote 26.

to pretend to accept his conditions. Or again, suppose I have genuinely promised someone that for the space of twenty days I will not taste food or any nourishment; and suppose I afterwards find that was foolish, and cannot be kept without very great injury to myself; as I am bound by natural law and right to choose the least of two evils, I have complete right to break my compact, and act as if my promise had never been uttered. I say that I should have perfect natural right to do so, whether I was actuated by true and evident reason, or whether I was actuated by mere opinion in thinking I had promised rashly; whether my reasons were true or false, I should be in fear of a greater evil, which, by the ordinance of nature, I should strive to avoid by every means in my power.

We may, therefore, conclude that a compact is only made valid by its utility, without which it becomes null and void. It is, therefore, foolish to ask a man to keep his faith with us for ever, unless we also endeavour that the violation of the compact we enter into shall involve for the violator more harm than good. This consideration should have very great weight in forming a state. However, if all men could be easily led by reason alone, and could recognize what is best and most useful for a state, there would be no one who would not forswear deceit, for everyone would keep most religiously to their compact in their desire for the chief good, namely, the shield and buckler of the commonwealth. However, it is far from being the case that all men can always be easily led by reason alone; everyone is drawn away by his pleasure, while avarice, ambition, envy, hatred, and the like so engross the mind that, reason has no place therein. Hence, though men make—promises with all the appearances of good faith, and agree that they will keep to their engagement, no one can absolutely rely on another man's promise unless there is something behind it. Everyone has by nature a right to act deceitfully. and to break his compacts, unless he be restrained by the hope of some greater good, or the fear of some greater evil.

However, as we have shown that the natural right of the individual is only limited by his power, it is clear that by transferring, either willingly or under compulsion, this power into the hands of another, he in so doing necessarily cedes also a part of his right; and further, that the Sovereign right over all men belongs to him who has sovereign power, wherewith he can compel men by force, or restrain them by threats of the universally feared punishment of death; such sovereign right he will retain only so long as he can maintain his power of enforcing his will; otherwise he will totter on his throne, and no one who is stronger than he will be bound unwillingly to obey him.

In this manner a society can be formed without any violation of natural right, and the covenant can always be strictly kept—that is, if each individual hands over the whole of his power to the body politic, the latter will then possess sovereign natural right over all things; that is, it will have sole and unquestioned dominion, and everyone will be bound to obey, under pain of the severest punishment. A body politic of this kind is called a Democracy, which may be defined as a society which wields all its power as a whole. The sovereign power is not restrained by any laws, but everyone is bound to obey it in all things; such is the state of things implied when men either tacitly or expressly handed over to it all their power of self-defence, or in other words, all their right. For if they had wished to retain any right for themselves, they ought to have taken precautions for its defence and preservation; as they have not done so, and indeed could not have done so without dividing and consequently ruining the state, they placed themselves absolutely at the mercy of the sovereign power; and, therefore, having acted (as we have shown) as reason and necessity demanded, they are obliged to fulfil the commands of the sovereign power, however absurd these may be, else they will be public enemies, and will act against reason, which urges the preservation of the state as a primary duty. For reason bids us choose the least of two evils.

Furthermore, this danger of submitting absolutely to the dominion and will of another, is one which may be incurred with a light heart: for we have shown that sovereigns only possess this right of imposing their will, so long as they have the full power to enforce it: if such power be lost their right to command is lost also, or lapses to those who have assumed it and can keep it. Thus it is very rare for sovereigns to impose thoroughly irrational commands, for they are bound to consult their own interests, and retain their power by consulting the public good and acting according to the dictates of reason, as Seneca says, "violenta imperia nemo continuit diu." No one can long retain a tyrant's sway.

In a democracy, irrational commands are still less to be feared: for it is almost impossible that the majority of a people, especially if it be a large one, should agree in an irrational design: and, moreover, the basis and aim of a democracy is to avoid the desires as irrational, and to bring men as far as possible under the control of reason, so that they may live in peace and harmony: if this basis be removed the whole fabric falls to ruin.

Such being the ends in view for the sovereign power, the duty of subjects is, as I have said, to obey its commands, and to recognize no right save that which it sanctions.

It will, perhaps, be thought that we are turning subjects into slaves: for slaves obey commands and free men live as they like; but this idea is based on a misconception, for the true slave is he who is led away by his pleasures and can neither see what is good for him nor act accordingly: he alone is free who lives with free consent under the entire guidance of reason.

Action in obedience to orders does take away freedom in a certain sense, but it does not, therefore, make a man a slave, all depends on the object of the action. If the object of the action be the good of the state, and not the good of the agent, the latter is a slave and does himself no good: but in a state or kingdom where the weal of the whole people, and not that of the ruler, is the supreme law, obedience to the sovereign power does not make a man a slave, of no use to himself, but a subject. Therefore, that state is the freest whose laws are founded on sound reason, so that every member of it may, if he will, be free;[2] that is, live with full consent under the entire guidance of reason.

---

2   See Endnote 27.

Children, though they are bound to obey all the commands of their parents, are yet not slaves: for the commands of parents look generally to the children's benefit.

We must, therefore, acknowledge a great difference between a slave, a son, and a subject; their positions may be thus defined. A slave is one who is bound to obey his master's orders, though they are given solely in the master's interest: a son is one who obeys his father's orders, given in his own interest; a subject obeys the orders of the sovereign power, given for the common interest, wherein he is included.

I think I have now shown sufficiently clearly the basis of a democracy: I have especially desired to do so, for I believe it to be of all forms of government the most natural, and the most consonant with individual liberty. In it no one transfers his natural right so absolutely that he has no further voice in affairs, he only hands it over to the majority of a society, whereof he is a unit. Thus all men remain as they were in the state of nature, equals.

This is the only form of government which I have treated of at length, for it is the one most akin to my purpose of showing the benefits of freedom in a state.

I may pass over the fundamental principles of other forms of government, for we may gather from what has been said whence their right arises without going into its origin. The possessor of sovereign power, whether he be one, or many, or the whole body politic, has the sovereign right of imposing any commands he pleases: and he who has either voluntarily, or under compulsion, transferred the right to defend him to another, has, in so doing, renounced his natural right and is therefore bound to obey, in all things, the commands of the sovereign power; and will be bound so to do so long as the king, or nobles, or the people preserve the sovereign power which formed the basis of the original transfer. I need add no more.

The bases and rights of dominion being thus displayed, we shall readily be able to define private civil right, wrong, justice, and injustice, with their relations to the state; and also to determine what constitutes an ally, or an enemy, or the crime of treason.

By private civil right we can only mean the liberty every man possesses to preserve his existence, a liberty limited by the edicts of the sovereign power, and preserved only by its authority: for when a man has transferred to another his right of living as he likes, which was only limited by his power, that is, has transferred his liberty and power of self-defence, he is bound to live as that other dictates, and to trust to him entirely for his defence. Wrong takes place when a citizen, or subject, is forced by another to undergo some loss or pain in contradiction to the authority of the law, or the edict of the sovereign power.

Wrong is conceivable only in an organized community: nor can it ever accrue to subjects from any act of the sovereign, who has the right to do what he likes. It can only arise, therefore, between private persons, who are bound by law and right not to injure one another. Justice consists in the habitual rendering to every man his lawful due: injustice consists in depriving a man, under the pretence of legality, of what the laws, rightly interpreted, would allow him. These last are also called equity and iniquity, because those who administer the laws are bound to show no respect of persons, but to account all men equal, and to defend every man's right equally, neither envying the rich nor despising the poor.

The men of two states become allies, when for the sake of avoiding war, or for some other advantage, they covenant to do each other no hurt, but on the contrary, to assist each other if necessity arises, each retaining his independence. Such a covenant is valid so long as its basis of danger or advantage is in force: no one enters into an engagement, or is bound to stand by his compacts unless there be a hope of some accruing good, or the fear of some evil: if this basis be removed the compact thereby becomes void: this has been abundantly shown by experience. For although different states make treaties not to harm one another, they always take every possible precaution against such treaties being broken by the stronger party, and do not rely on the compact, unless there is a sufficiently obvious object and advantage to both parties in observing it. Otherwise they would fear a breach of faith, nor would there be any wrong done thereby: for who in his proper senses, and aware of the right of the sovereign power, would trust in the promises of one who has the will and the power to do what he likes, and who aims solely at the safety and advantage of his dominion? Moreover, if we consult loyalty and religion, we shall see that no one in possession of power ought to abide by his promises to the injury of his dominion; for he cannot keep such promises without breaking the engagement he made with his subjects, by which both he and they are most solemnly bound. An enemy is one who lives apart from the state, and does not recognize its authority either as a subject or as an ally. It is not hatred which makes a man an enemy, but the rights of the state. The rights of the state are the same in regard to him who does not recognize by any compact the state authority, as they are against him who has done the state an injury: it has the right to force him as best it can, either to submit, or to contract an alliance.

Lastly, treason can only be committed by subjects, who by compact, either tacit or expressed, have transferred all their rights to the state: a subject is said to have committed this crime when he has attempted, for whatever reason, to seize the sovereign power, or to place it in different hands. I say, has attempted, for if punishment were not to overtake him till he had succeeded, it would often come too late, the sovereign rights would have been acquired or transferred already.

I also say, has attempted, for whatever reason, to seize the sovereign power, and I recognize no difference whether such an attempt should be followed by public loss or public gain. Whatever be his reason for acting, the crime is treason, and he is rightly condemned: in war, everyone would admit the justice of his sentence. If a man does not keep to his post, but approaches the enemy without the knowledge of his commander, whatever may be his motive, so long as he acts on his own motion, even if he advances with the design of defeating the enemy, he is rightly put to death, because he has violated his oath, and infringed the rights of his commander. That all citizens are equally bound by these rights in time of peace, is not so generally recognized, but the reasons for obedience are in both cases identical. The state must be preserved and directed by the sole authority of the sovereign, and such authority and right have been accorded by universal consent to him alone: if, therefore, anyone else attempts, without his consent, to execute any public enterprise, even though the state might (as we said) reap benefit therefrom, such person has none the less infringed the sovereigns right, and would be rightly punished for treason.

In order that every scruple may be removed, we may now answer the inquiry, whether our former assertion that everyone who has not the practice of reason, may, in the state of nature, live by sovereign natural right, according to the laws of his desires, is not in direct opposition to the law and right of God as revealed. For as all men absolutely (whether they be less endowed with reason or more) are equally bound by the Divine command to love their neighbour as themselves, it may be said that they cannot, without wrong, do injury to anyone, or live according to their desires.

This objection, so far as the state of nature is concerned, can be easily answered, for the state of nature is, both in nature and in time, prior to religion. No one knows by nature that he owes any obedience to God,[3] nor can he attain thereto by any exercise of his reason, but solely by revelation confirmed by signs. Therefore, previous to revelation, no one is bound by a Divine law and right of which he is necessarily in ignorance. The state of nature must by no means be confounded with a state of religion, but must be conceived as without either religion or law, and consequently without sin or wrong: this is how we have described it, and we are confirmed by the authority of Paul. It is not only in respect of ignorance that we conceive the state of nature as prior to, and lacking the Divine revealed law and right; but in respect of freedom also, wherewith all men are born endowed.

---

3   See Endnote 28.

If men were naturally bound by the Divine law and right, or if the Divine law and right were a natural necessity, there would have been no need for God to make a covenant with mankind, and to bind them thereto with an oath and agreement.

We must, then, fully grant that the Divine law and right originated at the time when men by express covenant agreed to obey God in all things, and ceded, as it were, their natural freedom, transferring their rights to God in the manner described in speaking of the formation of a state.

However, I will treat of these matters more at length presently.

It may be insisted that sovereigns are as much bound by the Divine law as subjects: whereas we have asserted that they retain their natural rights, and may do whatever they like.

In order to clear up the whole difficulty, which arises rather concerning the natural right than the natural state, I maintain that everyone is bound, in the state of nature, to live according to Divine law, in the same way as he is bound to live according to the dictates of sound reason; namely, inasmuch as it is to his advantage, and necessary for his salvation; but, if he will not so live, he may do otherwise at his own risk. He is thus bound to live according to his own laws, not according to anyone else's, and to recognize no man as a judge, or as a superior in religion. Such, in my opinion, is the position of a sovereign, for he may take advice from his fellow-men, but he is not bound to recognize any as a judge, nor anyone besides himself as an arbitrator on any question of right, unless it be a prophet sent expressly by God and attesting his mission by indisputable signs. Even then he does not recognize a man, but God Himself as His judge.

If a sovereign refuses to obey God as revealed in His law, he does so at his own risk and loss, but without violating any civil or natural right. For the civil right is dependent on his own decree; and natural right is dependent on the laws of nature, which latter are not adapted to religion, whose sole aim is the good of humanity, but to the order of nature—that is, to God's eternal decree unknown to us.

This truth seems to be adumbrated in a somewhat obscurer form by those who maintain that men can sin against God's revelation, but not against the eternal decree by which He has ordained all things.

We may be asked, what should we do if the sovereign commands anything contrary to religion, and the obedience which we have expressly vowed to God? should we obey the Divine law or the human law? I shall treat of this question at length hereafter, and will therefore merely say now, that God should be obeyed before all else, when we have a certain and indisputable revelation of His will: but men are very prone to error on religious subjects, and, according to the diversity of their dispositions, are wont with considerable stir to put forward their own inventions, as experience more than sufficiently attests, so that if no one were bound to obey the state in matters which, in his own opinion concern religion, the rights of the state would be dependent on every man's judgment and passions. No one would consider himself bound to obey laws framed against his faith or superstition; and on this pretext he might assume unbounded license. In this way, the rights of the civil authorities would be utterly set at nought, so that we must conclude that the sovereign power, which alone is bound both by Divine and natural right to preserve and guard the laws of the state, should have supreme authority for making any laws about religion which it thinks fit; all are bound to obey its behests on the subject in accordance with their promise which God bids them to keep.

However, if the sovereign power be heathen, we should either enter into no engagements therewith, and yield up our lives sooner than transfer to it any of our rights; or, if the engagement be made, and our rights transferred, we should (inasmuch as we should have ourselves transferred the right of defending ourselves and our religion) be bound to obey them, and to keep our word: we might even rightly be bound so to do, except in those cases where God, by indisputable revelation, has promised His special aid against tyranny, or given us special exemption from obedience. Thus we see that, of all the Jews in Babylon, there were only three youths who were certain of the help of God, and, therefore, refused to obey Nebuchadnezzar. All the rest, with the sole exception of Daniel, who was beloved by the king, were doubtless compelled by right to obey, perhaps thinking that they had been delivered up by God into the hands of the king, and that the king had obtained and preserved his dominion by God's design. On the other hand, Eleazar, before his country had utterly fallen, wished to give a proof of his constancy to his compatriots, in order that they might follow in his footsteps, and go to any lengths, rather than allow their right and power to be transferred to the Greeks, or brave any torture rather than swear allegiance to the heathen. Instances are occurring every day in confirmation of what I here advance. The rulers of Christian kingdoms do not hesitate, with a view to strengthening their dominion, to make treaties with Turks and heathen, and to give orders to their subjects who settle among such peoples not to assume more freedom, either in things secular or religious, than is set down in the treaty, or allowed by the foreign government. We may see this exemplified in the Dutch treaty with the Japanese, which I have already mentioned.

CHAPTER XVII

It is Shown That No One Can, or Need, Transfer All His Rights to the Sovereign Power. Of the Hebrew Republic, as it Was During the Lifetime of Moses, And After His Death, Till the Foundation of the Monarchy; And of its Excellence. Lastly, of the Causes Why the Theocratic Republic Fell, and Why it Could Hardly Have Continued Without Dissension.

THE theory put forward in the last chapter, of the universal rights of the sovereign power, and of the natural rights of the individual transferred thereto, though it corresponds in many respects with actual practice, and though practice may be so arranged as to conform to it more and more, must nevertheless always remain in many respects purely ideal. No one can ever so utterly transfer to another his power and, consequently, his rights, as to cease to be a man; nor can there ever be a power so sovereign that it can carry out every possible wish. It will always be vain to order a subject to hate what he believes brings him advantage, or to love what brings him loss, or not to be offended at insults, or not to wish to be free from fear, or a hundred other things of the sort, which necessarily follow from the laws of human nature. So much, I think, is abundantly shown by experience: for men have never so far ceded their power as to cease to be an object of fear to the rulers who received such power and right; and dominions have always been in as much danger from their own subjects as from external enemies. If it were really the case, that men could be deprived of their natural rights so utterly as never to have any further influence on affairs,[4] except with the permission of the holders

4   See Endnote 29.

of sovereign right, it would then be possible to maintain with impunity the most violent tyranny, which, I suppose, no one would for an instant admit.

We must, therefore, grant that every man retains some part of his right, in dependence on his own decision, and no one else's.

However, in order correctly to understand the extent of the sovereign's right and power, we must take notice that it does not cover only those actions to which it can compel men by fear, but absolutely every action which it can induce men to perform: for it is the fact of obedience, not the motive for obedience, which makes a man a subject.

Whatever be the cause which leads a man to obey the commands of the sovereign, whether it be fear or hope, or love of his country, or any other emotion—the fact remains that the man takes counsel with himself, and nevertheless acts as his sovereign orders. We must not, therefore, assert that all actions resulting from a man's deliberation with himself are done in obedience to the rights of the individual rather than the sovereign: as a matter of fact, all actions spring from a man's deliberation with himself, whether the determining motive be love or fear of punishment; therefore, either dominion does not exist, and has no rights over its subjects, or else it extends over every instance in which it can prevail on men to decide to obey it. Consequently, every action which a subject performs in accordance with the commands of the sovereign, whether such action springs from love, or fear, or (as is more frequently the case) from hope and fear together, or from reverence. compounded of fear and admiration, or, indeed, any motive whatever, is performed in virtue of his submission to the sovereign, and not in virtue of his own authority.

This point is made still more clear by the fact that obedience does not consist so much in the outward act as in the mental state of the person obeying; so that he is most under the dominion of another who with his whole heart determines to obey another's commands; and consequently the firmest dominion belongs to the sovereign who has most influence over the minds of his subjects; if those who are most feared possessed the firmest dominion, the firmest dominion would belong to the subjects of a tyrant, for they are always greatly feared by their ruler. Furthermore, though it is impossible to govern the mind as completely as the tongue, nevertheless minds are, to a certain extent, under the control of the sovereign, for he can in many ways bring about that the greatest part of his subjects should follow his wishes in their beliefs, their loves, and their hates. Though such emotions do not arise at the express command of the sovereign they often result (as experience shows) from the authority of his power, and from his direction ; in other words, in virtue of his right; we may, therefore, without doing violence to our understanding, conceive men who follow the instigation of their sovereign in their beliefs, their loves, their hates, their contempt, and all other emotions whatsoever.

Though the powers of government, as thus conceived, are sufficiently ample, they can never become large enough to execute every possible wish of their possessors. This, I think, I have already shown clearly enough. The method of forming a dominion which should prove lasting I do not, as I have said, intend to discuss, but in order to arrive at the object I have in view, I will touch on the teaching of Divine revelation to Moses in this respect, and we will consider the history and the success of the Jews, gathering therefrom what should be the chief concessions made by sovereigns to their subjects with a view to the security and increase of their dominion.

That the preservation of a state chiefly depends on the subjects' fidelity and constancy in carrying out the orders they receive, is most clearly taught both by reason and experience; how subjects ought to be guided so as best to preserve their fidelity and virtue is not so obvious. All, both rulers and ruled, are men, and prone to follow after their lusts. The fickle disposition of the multitude almost reduces those who have experience of it to despair, for it is governed solely by emotions, not by reason: it rushes headlong into every enterprise, and is easily corrupted either by avarice or luxury: everyone thinks himself omniscient and wishes to fashion all things to his liking, judging a thing to be just or unjust, lawful or unlawful, according as he thinks it will bring him profit or loss: vanity leads him to despise his equals, and refuse their guidance: envy of superior fame or fortune (for such gifts are never equally distributed) leads him to desire and rejoice in his neighbour's downfall. I need not go through the whole list, everyone knows already how much crime. results from disgust at the present—desire for change, headlong anger, and contempt for poverty—and how men's minds are engrossed and kept in turmoil thereby.

To guard against all these evils, and form a dominion where no room is left for deceit; to frame our institutions so that every man, whatever his disposition, may prefer public right to private advantage, this is the task and this the toil. Necessity is often the mother of invention, but she has never yet succeeded in framing a dominion that was in less danger from its own citizens than from open enemies, or whose rulers did not fear the latter less than the former. Witness the state of Rome, invincible by her enemies, but many times conquered and sorely oppressed by her own citizens, especially in the war between Vespasian and Vitellius. (See Tacitus, Hist. bk. iv. for a description of the pitiable state of the city.)

Alexander thought prestige abroad more easy to acquire than prestige at home, and believed that his greatness could be destroyed by his own followers. Fearing such a disaster, he thus addressed his friends: "Keep me safe from internal treachery and domestic plots, and I will front without fear the dangers of battle and of war. Philip was more secure in the battle array than in the theatre: he often escaped from the hands of the enemy, he could not escape from his own subjects. If you think over the deaths of kings, you will count up more who have died by the assassin than by the open foe." (Q. Curtius, chap. vi.)

For the sake of making themselves secure, kings who seized the throne in ancient times used to try to spread the idea that they were descended from the immortal gods, thinking that if their subjects and the rest of mankind did not look on them as equals, but believed them to be gods, they would willingly submit to their rule, and obey their commands. Thus Augustus persuaded the Romans that he was descended from AEneas, who was the son of Venus, and numbered among the gods. "He wished himself to be worshipped in temples, like the gods, with flamens and priests." (Tacitus, Ann. i. 10.)

Alexander wished to be saluted as the son of Jupiter, not from motives of pride but of policy, as he showed by his answer to the invective of Hermolaus: "It is almost laughable," said he, that Hermolaus asked me to contradict Jupiter, by whose oracle I am recognized. Am I responsible for the answers of the gods? It offered me the name of son; acquiescence was by no means foreign to my present designs. Would that the Indians also would believe me to be a god! Wars are carried through by prestige, falsehoods that are believed often gain the force of truth." (Curtius, viii,. Para, 8.) In these few words he cleverly contrives to palm off a fiction on the ignorant, and at the same time hints at the motive for the deception.

Cleon, in his speech persuading the Macedonians to obey their king, adopted a similar device: for after going through the praises of Alexander with admiration, and recalling his merits, he proceeds, "the Persians are not only pious, but prudent in worshipping their kings as gods: for kingship is the shield of public safety," and he ends thus, "I, myself, when the king enters a banquet hall, should prostrate my body on the ground; other men should do the like, especially those who are wise " (Curtius, viii. Para. 66). However, the Macedonians were more prudent—indeed, it is only complete barbarians who can be so openly cajoled, and can suffer themselves to be turned from subjects into slaves without interests of their own. Others, notwithstanding, have been able more easily to spread the belief that kingship is sacred, and plays the part of God on the earth, that it has been instituted by God, not by the suffrage and consent of men; and that it is preserved and guarded by Divine special providence and aid. Similar fictions have been promulgated by monarchs, with the object of strengthening their dominion, but these I will pass over, and in order to arrive at my main purpose, will merely recall and discuss the teaching on the subject of Divine revelation to Moses in ancient times.

We have said in Chap. v. that after the Hebrews came up out of Egypt they were not bound by the law and right of any other nation, but were at liberty to institute any new rites at their pleasure, and to occupy whatever territory they chose. After their liberation from the intolerable bondage of the Egyptians, they were bound by no covenant to any man; and, therefore, every man entered into his natural right, and was free to retain it or to give it up, and transfer it to another. Being, then, in the state of nature, they followed the advice of Moses, in whom they chiefly trusted, and decided to transfer their right to no human being, but only to God; without further delay they all, with one voice, promised to obey all the commands of the Deity, and to acknowledge no right that He did not proclaim as such by prophetic revelation. This promise, or transference of right to God, was effected in the same manner as we have conceived it to have been in ordinary societies, when men agree to divest themselves of their natural rights. It is, in fact, in virtue of a set covenant, and an oath (see Exod. xxxiv:10), that the Jews freely, and not under compulsion or threats, surrendered their rights and transferred them to God. Moreover, in order that this covenant might be ratified and settled, and might be free from all suspicion of deceit, God did not enter into it till the Jews had had experience of His wonderful power by which alone they had been, or could be, preserved in a state of prosperity (Exod. xix:4, 5). It is because they believed that nothing but God's power could preserve them that they surrendered to God the natural power of self-preservation, which they formerly, perhaps, thought they possessed, and consequently they surrendered at the same time all their natural right.

God alone, therefore, held dominion over the Hebrews, whose state was in virtue of the covenant called God's kingdom, and God was said to be their king; consequently the enemies of the Jews were said to be the enemies of God, and the citizens who tried to seize the dominion were guilty of treason against God; and, lastly, the laws of the state were called the laws and commandments of God. Thus in the Hebrew state the civil and religious authority, each consisting solely of obedience to God, were one and the same. The dogmas of religion were not precepts, but laws and ordinances; piety was regarded as the same as loyalty, impiety as the same as disaffection. Everyone who fell away from religion ceased to be a citizen, and was, on that ground alone, accounted an enemy: those who died for the sake of religion, were held to have died for their country; in fact, between civil and religious law and right there was no distinction whatever. {in Biblical Hebrew, there was no word for what we call Religion." Modern Hebrew has selected a word whose root is "knowledge."} For this reason the government could be called a Theocracy, inasmuch as the citizens were not bound by anything save the revelations of God.

However, this state of things existed rather in theory than in practice, for it will appear from what we are about to say, that the Hebrews, as a matter of fact, retained absolutely in their own hands the right of sovereignty: this is shown by the method and plan by which the government was carried on, as I will now explain.

Inasmuch as the Hebrews did not transfer their rights to any other person but, as in a democracy, all surrendered their rights equally, and cried out with one voice, "Whatsoever God shall speak (no mediator or mouthpiece being named) that will we do," it follows that all were equally bound by the covenant, and that all had an equal right to consult the Deity, to accept and to interpret His laws, so that all had an exactly equal share in the government. Thus at first they all approached God together, so that they might learn His commands, but in this first salutation, they were so thoroughly terrified and so astounded to hear God speaking, that they thought their last hour was at hand: full of fear, therefore, they went afresh to Moses, and said, "Lo, we have heard God speaking in the fire, and there is no cause why we should wish to die: surely this great fire will consume us: if we hear again the voice of God, we shall surely die. Thou, therefore, go near, and hear all the words of our God, and thou (not God) shalt speak with us: all that God shall tell us, that will we hearken to and perform."

They thus clearly abrogated their former covenant, and absolutely transferred to Moses their right to consult God and interpret His commands: for they do not here promise obedience to all that God shall tell them, but to all that God shall tell Moses (see Deut. v:20 after the Decalogue, and chap. xviii:15, 16). Moses, therefore, remained the sole promulgator and interpreter of the Divine laws, and consequently also the sovereign judge, who could not be arraigned himself, and who acted among the Hebrews the part, of God; in other words, held the sovereign kingship: he alone had the right to consult God, to give the Divine answers to the people, and to see that they were carried out. I say he alone, for if anyone during the life of Moses was desirous of preaching anything in the name of the Lord, he was, even if a true prophet, considered guilty and a usurper of the sovereign right (Numb. xi:28).[5] We may here notice, that though the people had elected Moses, they could not rightfully elect Moses's successor; for having transferred to Moses their right of consulting God, and absolutely promised to regard him as a Divine oracle, they had plainly forfeited the whole of their right, and were bound to accept as chosen by God anyone proclaimed by Moses as his successor. If Moses had so chosen his successor, who like him should wield the sole right of government, possessing the sole right of consulting God, and consequently of making and abrogating laws, of deciding on peace or war, of sending ambassadors, appointing judges—in fact, discharging all the functions of a sovereign, the state would have become simply a monarchy, only differing from other monarchies in the fact, that the latter are, or should be, carried on in accordance with God's decree, unknown even to the monarch, whereas the Hebrew monarch would have been the only person to whom the decree was revealed. A difference which increases, rather than diminishes the monarch's authority. As far as the people in both cases are concerned, each would be equally subject, and equally ignorant of the Divine decree, for each would be dependent on the monarch's words, and would learn from him alone, what was lawful or unlawful: nor would the fact that the people believed that the monarch

---

5   See Endnote 30.

was only issuing commands in accordance with God's decree revealed to him, make it less in subjection, but rather more. However, Moses elected no such successor, but left the dominion to those who came after him in a condition which could not be called a popular government, nor an aristocracy, nor a monarchy, but a Theocracy. For the right of interpreting laws was vested in one man, while the right and power of administering the state according to the laws thus interpreted, was vested in another man (see Numb. xxvii:21).[6]

In order that the question may be thoroughly understood, I will duly set forth the administration of the whole state.

First, the people were commanded to build a tabernacle, which should be, as it were, the dwelling of God—that is, of the sovereign authority of the state. This tabernacle was to be erected at the cost of the whole people, not of one man, in order that the place where God was consulted might be public property. The Levites were chosen as courtiers and administrators of this royal abode; while Aaron, the brother of Moses, was chosen to be their chief and second, as it were, to God their King, being succeeded in the office by his legitimate sons.

He, as the nearest to God, was the sovereign interpreter of the Divine laws; he communicated the answers of the Divine oracle to the people, and entreated God's favour for them. If, in addition to these privileges, he had possessed the right of ruling, he would have been neither more nor less than an absolute monarch; but, in respect to government, he was only a private citizen: the whole tribe of Levi was so completely divested of governing rights that it did not even take its share with the others in the partition of territory. Moses provided for its support by inspiring the common people with great reverence for it, as the only tribe dedicated to God.

Further, the army, formed from the remaining twelve tribes, was commanded to invade the land of Canaan, to divide it into twelve portions, and to distribute it among the tribes by lot. For this task twelve captains were chosen, one from every

---

6   See Endnote 31.

tribe, and were, together with Joshua and Eleazar, the high priest, empowered to divide the land into twelve equal parts, and distribute it by lot. Joshua was chosen for the chief command of the army, inasmuch as none but he had the right to consult God in emergencies, not like Moses, alone in his tent, or in the tabernacle, but through the high priest, to whom only the answers of God were revealed. Furthermore, he was empowered to execute, and cause the people to obey God's commands, transmitted through the high priests; to find, and to make use of, means for carrying them out; to choose as many, army captains as he liked; to make whatever choice he thought best; to send ambassadors in his own name; and, in short, to have the entire control of the war. To his office there was no rightful successor—indeed, the post was only filled by the direct order of the Deity, on occasions of public emergency. In ordinary times, all the management of peace and war was vested in the captains of the tribes, as I will shortly point out. Lastly, all men between the ages of twenty and sixty were ordered to bear arms, and form a citizen army, owing allegiance, not to its general-in-chief, nor to the high priest, but to Religion and to God. The army, or the hosts, were called the army of God, or the hosts of God. For this reason God was called by the Hebrews the God of Armies; and the ark of the covenant was borne in the midst of the army in important battles, when the safety or destruction of the whole people hung upon the issue, so that the people might, as it were, see their King among them, and put forth all their strength.

From these directions, left by Moses to his successors, we plainly see that he chose administrators, rather than despots, to come after him; for he invested no one with the power of consulting God, where he liked and alone, consequently, no one had the power possessed by himself of ordaining and abrogating laws, of deciding on war or peace, of choosing men to fill offices both religious and secular: all these are the prerogatives of a sovereign. The high priest, indeed, had the right of interpreting laws, and communicating the answers of God, but he could not do so when he liked, as Moses could, but only when he was asked by the general-in-chief of the army, the council, or some similar authority. The general-in-chief and the council could consult God when they liked, but could only receive His answers through the high priest; so that the utterances of God, as reported by the high priest, were not decrees, as they were when reported by Moses, but only answers; they were accepted by Joshua and the council, and only then had the force of commands and decrees {Like the separation of powers in the United States of America.}

The high priest, both in the case of Aaron and of his son Eleazar, was chosen by Moses; nor had anyone, after Moses' death, a right to elect to the office, which became hereditary . The general-in-chief of the army was also chosen by Moses, and assumed his functions in virtue of the commands, not of the high priest, but of Moses: indeed, after the death of Joshua, the high priest did not appoint anyone in his place, and the captains did not consult God afresh about a general-in-chief, but each retained Joshua's power in respect to the contingent of his own tribe, and all retained it collectively, in respect to the whole army. There seems to have been no need of a general-in-chief, except when they were obliged to unite their forces against a common enemy. This occurred most frequently during the time of Joshua, when they had no fixed dwelling. place, and possessed all things in common. After all the tribes had gained their territories by right of conquest, and had divided their allotted gains, they, became separated, having no longer their possessions in common, so that the need for a single commander ceased, for the different tribes should be considered rather in the light of confederated states than of bodies of fellow-citizens. In respect to their God and their religion, they, were fellow-citizens; but, in respect to the rights which one possessed with regard to another, they were only confederated: they, were, in fact, in much the same position (if one excepts the Temple common to all) as the United States of the Netherlands {or United States of America}. The division of property, held in common is only another phrase for the possession of his share by each of the owners singly, and the surrender by the others of their rights over such share. This is why Moses elected captains of the tribes—namely, that when the dominion was divided, each might take care of his own part; consulting God through the high priest on the affairs of his tribe, ruling over his army, building and fortifying cities, appointing judges, attacking the enemies of his own dominion, and having complete control over all civil and military affairs. He was not bound to acknowledge any superior judge save God,[7] or a prophet whom God should expressly send. If he departed from the worship of God, the rest of the tribes did not arraign him as a subject, but attacked him as an enemy. Of this we have examples in Scripture. When Joshua was dead, the children of Israel (not a fresh general-in-chief) consulted God; it being decided that the tribe of Judah should be the first to attack its enemies, the tribe in question contracted a single alliance with the tribe of Simeon, for uniting their forces, and attacking their common enemy, the rest of the tribes not being included in the alliance (Judges i:1, 2, 3). Each tribe separately made war against its own enemies, and, according to its pleasure, received them as subjects or allies, though it had been commanded not to spare them on any conditions, but to destroy them utterly. Such disobedience met with reproof from the rest of the tribes, but did not cause the offending tribe to be arraigned: it was not considered a sufficient reason for proclaiming a civil war, or interfering in one another's affairs. But when the tribe of Benjamin offended against the others, and so loosened the bonds of peace that none of the confederated tribes could find refuge within its borders, they attacked it as an enemy, and gaining the victory over it after three battles, put to death both guilty and innocent, according to the laws of war: an act which they subsequently bewailed with tardy repentance.

These examples plainly confirm what we have said concerning the rights of each tribe. Perhaps we shall be asked who elected the successors to the captains of each tribe; on this point I can gather no positive information in Scripture, but I conjecture that as the tribes were divided into families, each headed by its senior member, the senior of all these heads of families succeeded by right to the office of captain, for Moses

7   See Endnote 32.

chose from among these seniors his seventy coadjutors, who formed with himself the supreme council. Those who administered the government after the death of Joshua were called elders, and elder is a very common Hebrew expression in the sense of judge, as I suppose everyone knows; however, it is not very important for us to make up our minds on this point. It is enough to have shown that after the death of Moses no one man wielded all the power of a sovereign; as affairs were not all managed by one man, nor by a single council, nor by the popular vote, but partly by one tribe, partly by the rest in equal shares, it is most evident that the government, after the death of Moses, was neither monarchic, nor aristocratic, nor popular, but, as we have said, Theocratic. The reasons for applying this name are:

I.   Because the royal seat of government was the Temple, and in respect to it alone, as we have shown, all the tribes were fellow-citizens,

II. Because all the people owed allegiance to God, their supreme Judge, to whom only they had promised implicit obedience in all things.

III. Because the general-in-chief or dictator, when there was need of such, was elected by none save God alone. This was expressly commanded by Moses in the name of God (Deut. xix:15), and witnessed by the actual choice of Gideon, of Samson, and of Samuel; wherefrom we may conclude that the other faithful leaders were chosen in the same manner, though it is not expressly told us.

These preliminaries being stated, it is now time to inquire the effects of forming a dominion on this plan, and to see whether it so effectually kept within bounds both rulers and ruled, that the former were never tyrannical and the latter never rebellious.

Those who administer or possess governing power, always try to surround their high-handed actions with a cloak of legality, and to persuade the people that they act from good motives; this they are easily able to effect when they are the sole interpreters of the law; for it is evident that they are thus able to assume a far greater freedom to carry out their wishes and desires than if the interpretation if the law is vested in someone else, or if the laws were so self-evident that no one could be in doubt as to their meaning. We thus see that the power of evil—doing was greatly curtailed for the Hebrew captains by the fact that the whole interpretation of the law was vested in the Levites (Deut. xxi:5), who, on their part, had no share in the government, and depended for all their support and consideration on a correct interpretation of the laws entrusted to them. Moreover, the whole people was commanded to come together at a certain place every seven years and be instructed in the law by the high-priest; further, each individual was bidden to read the book of the law through and through continually with scrupulous care. (Deut. xxxi:9, 10, and vi:7.) The captains were thus for their own sakes bound to take great care to administer everything according to the laws laid down, and well known to all, if they, wished to be held in high honour by, the people, who would regard them as the administrators of God's dominion, and as God's vicegerents; otherwise they could not have escaped all the virulence of theological hatred. There was another very important check on the unbridled license of the captains, in the fact, that the army was formed from the whole body, of the citizens, between the ages of twenty and sixty, without exception, and that the captains were not able to hire any foreign soldiery. This I say was very, important, for it is well known that princes can oppress their peoples with the single aid of the soldiery in their pay; while there is nothing more formidable to them than the freedom of citizen soldiers, who have established the freedom and glory of their country, by their valour, their toil, and their blood. Thus Alexander, when he was about to make wax on Darius, a second time, after hearing the advice of Parmenio, did not chide him who gave the advice, but Polysperchon, who was standing by. For, as Curtius says (iv. Para. 13), he did not venture to reproach Parmenio again after having shortly, before reproved him too sharply. This freedom of the Macedonians, which he so dreaded, he was not able to subdue till after the number of captives enlisted in the army, surpassed that of his own people: then, but not till then, he gave rein to his anger so long checked by, the independence of his chief fellow-countrymen.

If this independence of citizen soldiers can restrain the princes of ordinary states who are wont to usurp the whole glory of victories, it must have been still more effectual against the Hebrew captains, whose soldiers were fighting, not for the glory of a prince, but for the glory of God, and who did not go forth to battle till the Divine assent had been given.

We must also remember that the Hebrew captains were associated only by the bonds of religion: therefore, if any one of them had transgressed, and begun to violate the Divine right, he might have been treated by the rest as an enemy and lawfully subdued.

An additional check may be found in the fear of a new prophet arising, for if a man of unblemished life could show by certain signs that he was really a prophet, he ipso facto obtained the sovereign right to rule, which was given to him, as to Moses formerly, in the name of God, as revealed to himself alone; not merely through the high priest, as in the case of the captains. There is no doubt that such an one would easily be able to enlist an oppressed people in his cause, and by trifling signs persuade them of anything he wished: on the other hand, if affairs were well ordered, the captain would be able to make provision in time; that the prophet should be submitted to his approval, and be examined whether he were really of unblemished life, and possessed indisputable signs of his mission: also, whether the teaching he proposed to set forth in the name of the Lord agreed with received doctrines, and the general laws of the country; if his credentials were insufficient, or his doctrines new, he could lawfully be put to death, or else received on the captain's sole responsibility and authority.

Again, the captains were not superior to the others in nobility or birth, but only administered the government in virtue of their age and personal qualities. Lastly, neither captains nor army had any reason for preferring war to peace. The army, as we have stated, consisted entirely of citizens, so that affairs were managed by the same persons both in peace and war. The man who was a soldier in the camp was a citizen in the market-place, he who was a leader in the camp was a judge in the law courts, he who was a general in the camp was a ruler in the state. Thus no one could desire war for its own sake, but only for the sake of preserving peace and liberty; possibly the captains avoided change as far as possible, so as not to be obliged to consult the high priest and submit to the indignity of standing in his presence.

So much for the precautions for keeping the captains within bounds. We must now look for the restraints upon the people: these, however, are very clearly indicated in the very ground-work of the social fabric.

Anyone who gives the subject the slightest attention, will see that the state was so ordered as to inspire the most ardent patriotism in the hearts of the citizens, so that the latter would be very hard to persuade to betray their country, and be ready to endure anything rather than submit to a foreign yoke. After they had transferred their right to God, they thought that their kingdom belonged to God, and that they themselves were God's children. Other nations they looked upon as God's enemies, and regarded with intense hatred (which they took to be piety, see Psalm cxxxix:21, 22): nothing would have been more abhorrent to them than swearing allegiance to a foreigner, and promising him obedience: nor could they conceive any greater or more execrable crime than the betrayal of their country, the kingdom of the God whom they adored.

It was considered wicked for anyone to settle outside of the country, inasmuch as the worship of God by which they were bound could not be carried on elsewhere: their own land alone was considered holy, the rest of the earth unclean and profane.

David, who was forced to live in exile, complained before Saul as follows: "But if they be the children of men who have stirred thee up against me, cursed be they before the Lord; for they have driven me out this day from abiding in the inheritance of the Lord, saying, Go, serve other gods." (I Sam. xxvi:19.) For the same reason no citizen, as we should especially remark, was ever sent into exile: he who sinned was liable to punishment, but not to disgrace.

Thus the love of the Hebrews for their country was not only patriotism, but also piety, and was cherished and nurtured bv daily rites till, like their hatred of other nations, it must have passed into their nature. Their daily worship was not only different from that of other nations (as it might well be, considering that they were a peculiar people and entirely apart from the rest), it was absolutely contrary. Such daily reprobation naturally gave rise to a lasting hatred, deeply implanted in the heart: for of all hatreds none is more deep and tenacious than that which springs from extreme devoutness or piety, and is itself cherished as pious. Nor was a general cause lacking for inflaming such hatred more and more, inasmuch as it was reciprocated; the surrounding nations regarding the Jews with a hatred just as intense.

How great was the effect of all these causes, namely, freedom from man's dominion; devotion to their country; absolute rights over all other men; a hatred not only permitted but pious; a contempt for their fellow-men; the singularity of their customs and religious rites; the effect, I repeat, of all these causes in strengthening the hearts of the Jews to bear all things for their country, with extraordinary constancy and valour, will at once be discerned by reason and attested by experience. Never, so long as the city was standing, could they endure to remain under foreign dominion; and therefore they called Jerusalem "a rebellious city" (Ezra iv:12). Their state after its reestablishment (which was a mere shadow of the first, for the high priests had usurped the rights of the tribal captains) was, with great difficulty, destroyed by the Romans, as Tacitus bears witness (Hist. ii:4):—"Vespasian had closed the war against the Jews, abandoning the siege of Jerusalem as an enterprise difficult and arduous rather from the character of the people and the obstinacy of their superstition, than from the strength left to the besieged for meeting their necessities." But besides these characteristics, which are merely ascribed by an individual opinion, there was one feature peculiar to this state and of great importance in retaining the affections of the citizens, and checking all thoughts of desertion, or abandonment of the country: namely, self-interest, the strength and life of all human action. This was peculiarly engaged in the Hebrew state, for nowhere else did citizens possess their goods so securely, as did the subjects of this community, for the latter possessed as large a share in the land and the fields as did their chiefs, and were owners of their plots of ground in perpetuity; for if any man was compelled by poverty to sell his farm or his pasture, he received it back again intact at the year of jubilee: there were other similar enactments against the possibility of alienating real property.

Again, poverty w as nowhere more endurable than in a country where duty towards one's neighbour, that is, one's fellow-citizen, was practised with the utmost piety, as a means of gaining the favour of God the King. Thus the Hebrew citizens would nowhere be so well off as in their own country; outside its limits they met with nothing but loss and disgrace.

The following considerations were of weight, not only in keeping them at home, but also in preventing civil war and removing causes of strife; no one was bound to serve his equal, but only to serve God, while charity and love towards fellow-citizens was accounted the highest piety; this last feeling was not a little fostered by the general hatred with which they regarded foreign nations and were regarded by them. Furthermore, the strict discipline of obedience in which they were brought up, was a very important factor; for they were bound to carry on all their actions according to the set rules of the law: a man might not plough when he liked, but only at certain times, in certain years, and with one sort of beast at a time; so, too, he might only sow and reap in a certain method and season—in fact, his whole life was one long school of obedience (see Chap. V. on the use of ceremonies); such a habit was thus engendered, that conformity seemed freedom instead of servitude, and men desired what was commanded rather than what was forbidden. This result was not a little aided by the fact that the people were bound, at certain seasons of the year, to give themselves up to rest and rejoicing, not for their own pleasure, but in order that they might worship God cheerfully.

Three times in the year they feasted before the Lord; on the seventh day of every week they were bidden to abstain from all work and to rest; besides these, there were other occasions when innocent rejoicing and feasting were not only allowed but enjoined. I do not think any better means of influencing men's minds could be devised; for there is no more powerful attraction than joy springing from devotion, a mixture of admiration and love. It was not easy to be wearied by constant repetition, for the rites on the various festivals were varied and recurred seldom. We may add the deep reverence for the Temple which all most religiously fostered, on account of the peculiar rites and duties that they were obliged to perform before approaching thither. Even now, Jews cannot read without horror of the crime of Manasseh, who dared to place au idol in the Temple. The laws, scrupulously preserved in the inmost sanctuary, were objects of equal reverence to the people. Popular reports and misconceptions were, therefore, very little to be feared in this quarter, for no one dared decide on sacred matters, but all felt bound to obey, without consulting their reason, all the commands given by the answers of God received in the Temple, and all the laws which God had ordained.

I think I have now explained clearly, though briefly,, the main features of the Hebrew commonwealth. I must now inquire into the causes which led the people so often to fall away from the law, which brought about their frequent subjection, and, finally, the complete destruction of their dominion. Perhaps I shall be told that it sprang from their hardness of heart; but this is childish, for why should this people be more hard of heart than others; was it by nature?

But nature forms individuals, not peoples; the latter are only distinguishable by the difference of their language, their customs, and their laws; while from the two last—i.e., customs and laws,—it may arise that they have a peculiar disposition, a peculiar manner of life, and peculiar prejudices. If, then, the

Hebrews were harder of heart than other nations, the fault lay with their laws or customs.

This is certainly true, in the sense that, if God had wished their dominion to be more lasting, He would have given them other rites and laws, and would have instituted a different form of government. We can, therefore, only say that their God was angry with them, not only, as Jeremiah says, from the building of the city, but even from the founding of their laws.

This is borne witness to by Ezekiel xx:25: "Wherefore I gave them also statutes that were not good, and judgments whereby they should not live; and I polluted them in their own gifts, in that they caused to pass through the fire all that openeth the womb; that I might make them desolate, to the end that they might know that I am the Lord."

In order that we may understand these words, and the destruction of the Hebrew commonwealth, we must bear in mind that it had at first been intended to entrust the whole duties of the priesthood to the firstborn, and not to the Levites (see Numb. viii:17). It was only when all the tribes, except the Levites, worshipped the golden calf, that the firstborn were rejected and defiled, and the Levites chosen in their stead (Deut. x:8). When I reflect on this change, I feel disposed to break forth with the words of Tacitus. God's object at that time was not the safety of the Jews, but vengeance. I am greatly astonished that the celestial mind was so inflamed with anger that it ordained laws, which always are supposed to promote the honour, well-being, and security of a people, with the purpose of vengeance, for the sake of punishment; so that the laws do not seem so much laws—that is, the safeguard of the people—as pains and penalties.

The gifts which the people were obliged to bestow on the Levites and priests—the redemption of the firstborn, the poll-tax due to the Levites, the privilege possessed by the latter of the sole performance of sacred rites—all these, I say, were a continual reproach to the people, a continual reminder of their defilement and rejection. Moreover, we may be sure that the

Levites were for ever heaping reproaches upon them: for among so many thousands there must have been many importunate dabblers in theology. Hence the people got into the way of watching the acts of the Levites, who were but human; of accusing the whole body of the faults of one member, and continually murmuring.

Besides this, there was the obligation to keep in idleness men hateful to them, and connected by no ties of blood. Especially would this seem grievous when provisions were dear. What wonder, then, if in times of peace, when striking miracles had ceased, and no men of paramount authority were forthcoming, the irritable and greedy temper of the people began to wax cold, and at length to fall away from a worship, which, though Divine, was also humiliating, and even hostile, and to seek after something fresh; or can we be surprised that the captains, who always adopt the popular course, in order to gain the sovereign power for themselves by enlisting the sympathies of the people, and alienating the high priest, should have yielded to their demands, and introduced a new worship? If the state had been formed according to the original intention, the rights and honour of all the tribes would have been equal, and everything would have rested on a firm basis. Who is there who would willingly violate the religious rights of his kindred? What could a man desire more than to support his own brothers and parents, thus fulfilling the duties of religion? Who would not rejoice in being taught by them the interpretation of the laws, and receiving through them the answers of God?

The tribes would thus have been united by a far closer bond, if all alike had possessed the right to the priesthood. All danger would have been obviated, if the choice of the Levites had not been dictated by anger and revenge. But, as we have said, the Hebrews had offended their God, Who, as Ezekiel says, polluted them in their own gifts by rejecting all that openeth the womb, so that He might destroy them.

This passage is also confirmed by their history. As soon as the people in the wilderness began to live in ease and plenty, certain men of no mean birth began to rebel against the choice of the Levites, and to make it a cause for believing that Moses had not acted by the commands of God, but for his own good pleasure, inasmuch as he had chosen his own tribe before all the rest, and had bestowed the high priesthood in perpetuity on his own brother. They, therefore, stirred up a tumult, and came to him, crying out that all men were equally sacred, and that he had exalted himself above his fellows wrongfully. Moses was not able to pacify them with reasons; but by the intervention of a miracle in proof of the faith, they all perished. A fresh sedition then arose among the whole people, who believed that their champions had not been put to death by the judgment of God, but by the device of Moses. After a great slaughter, or pestilence, the rising subsided from inanition, but in such a manner that all preferred death to life under such conditions.

We should rather say that sedition ceased than that harmony was re-established. This is witnessed by Scripture (Deut. xxxi:21), where God, after predicting to Moses that the people after his death will fall away from the Divine worship, speaks thus: "For I know their imagination which they go about, even now before I have brought them into the land which I sware;" and, a little while after (xxxi:27), Moses says: For I know thy rebellion and thy stiff neck: behold while I am yet alive with you this day, ye have been rebellious against the Lord; and how much more after my death!"

Indeed, it happened according to his words, as we all know. Great changes, extreme license, luxury, and hardness of heart grew up; things went from bad to worse, till at last the people, after being frequently conquered, came to an open rupture with the Divine right, and wished for a mortal king, so that the seat of government might be the Court, instead of the Temple, and that the tribes might remain fellow-citizens in respect to their king, instead of in respect to Divine right and the high priesthood.

A vast material for new seditions was thus produced, eventually resulting in the ruin of the entire state. Kings are above all things jealous of a precarious rule, and can in nowise brook a dominion within their own. The first monarchs, being chosen from the ranks of private citizens, were content with the amount of dignity to which they had risen; but their sons, who obtained the throne by right of inheritance, began gradually to introduce changes, so as to get all the sovereign rights into their own hands. This they were generally unable to accomplish, so long as the right of legislation did not rest with them, but with the high priest, who kept the laws in the sanctuary, and interpreted them to the people. The kings were thus bound to obey the laws as much as were the subjects, and were unable to abrogate them, or to ordain new laws of equal authority; moreover, they were prevented by the Levites from administering the affairs of religion, king and subject being alike unclean. Lastly, the whole safety of their dominion depended on the will of one man, if that man appeared to be a prophet; and of this they had seen an example, namely, how completely Samuel had been able to command Saul, and how easily, because of a single disobedience, he had been able to transfer the right of sovereignty to David. Thus the kings found a dominion within their own, and wielded a precarious sovereignty.

In order to surmount these difficulties, they allowed other temples to be dedicated to the gods, so that there might be no further need of consulting the Levites; they also sought out many who prophesied in the name of God, so that they might have creatures of their own to oppose to the true prophets. However, in spite of all their attempts, they never attained their end. For the prophets, prepared against every emergency, waited for a favourable opportunity, such as the beginning of a new reign, which is always precarious, while the memory of the previous reign remains green. At these times they could easily pronounce by Divine authority that the king was tyrannical, and could produce a champion of distinguished virtue to vindicate the Divine right, and lawfully to claim dominion, or a share in it. Still, not even so could the prophets effect much. They could, indeed, remove a tyrant; but there were reasons which prevented them from doing more than setting up, at great cost of civil bloodshed, another tyrant in his stead. Of discords and civil wars there was no end, for the causes for the violation of Divine right remained always the same, and could only be removed by a complete remodelling of the state.

We have now seen how religion was introduced into the Hebrew commonwealth, and how the dominion might have lasted for ever, if the just wrath of the Lawgiver had allowed it. As this was impossible, it was bound in time to perish. I am now speaking only of the first commonwealth, for the second was a mere shadow of the first, inasmuch as the people were bound by the rights of the Persians to whom they were subject. After the restoration of freedom, the high priests usurped the rights of the secular chiefs, and thus obtained absolute dominion. The priests were inflamed with an intense desire to wield the powers of the sovereignty and the high priesthood at the same time. I have, therefore, no need to speak further of the second commonwealth. Whether the first, in so far as we deem it to have been durable, is capable of imitation, and whether it would be pious to copy it as far as possible, will appear from what fellows. I wish only to draw attention, as a crowning conclusion, to the principle indicated already—namely, that it is evident, from what we have stated in this chapter, that the Divine right, or the right of religion, originates in a compact: without such compact, none but natural rights exist. The Hebrews were not bound by their religion to evince any pious care for other nations not included in the compact, but only for their own fellow-citizens.

CHAPTER XVIII

From the Commonwealth of the Hebrews, And Their History, Certain Political Doctrines are Deduced.

ALTHOUGH the commonwealth of the Hebrews, as we have conceived it, might have lasted for ever, it would be impossible to imitate it at the present day, nor would it be advisable so to do. If a people wished to transfer their rights to God it would be necessary to make an express covenant with Him, and for this would be needed not only the consent of those transferring their rights, but also the consent of God. God, however, has revealed through his Apostles that the covenant of God is no longer written in ink, or on tables of stone, but with the Spirit of God in the fleshy tables of the heart.

Furthermore, such a form of government would only be available for those who desire to have no foreign relations, but to shut themselves up within their own frontiers, and to live apart from the rest of the world; it would be useless to men who must have dealings with other nations; so that the cases where it could be adopted are very few indeed.

Nevertheless, though it could not be copied in its entirety, it possessed many excellent features which might be brought to our notice, and perhaps imitated with advantage. My intention, however, is not to write a treatise on forms of government, so I will pass over most of such points in silence, and will only touch on those which bear upon my purpose.

God's kingdom is not infringed upon by the choice of an earthly ruler endowed with sovereign rights; for after the Hebrews had transferred their rights to God, they conferred the sovereign right of ruling on Moses, investing him with the sole power of instituting and abrogating laws in the name of God, of choosing priests, of judging, of teaching, of punishing—in fact, all the prerogatives of an absolute monarch.

Again, though the priests were the interpreters of the laws, they had no power to judge the citizens, or to excommunicate anyone: this could only be done by the judges and chiefs chosen from among the people. A consideration of the successes and the histories of the Hebrews will bring to light other considerations worthy of note. To wit:

I.   That there were no religious sects, till after the high priests, in the second commonwealth, possessed the authority to make decrees, and transact the business of government. In order that such authority might last for ever, the high priests usurped the rights of secular rulers, and at last wished to be styled kings. The reason for this is ready to hand; in the first commonwealth no decrees could bear the name of the high priest, for he had no right to ordain laws, but only to give the answers of God to questions asked by the captains or the councils: he had, therefore, no motive for making changes in the law, but took care, on the contrary, to administer and guard what had already been received and accepted. His only means of preserving his freedom in safety against the will of the captains lay in cherishing the law intact. After the high priests had assumed the power of carrying on the government, and added the rights of secular rulers to those they already possessed, each one began both in things religious and in things secular, to seek for the glorification of his own name, settling everything by sacerdotal authority, and issuing every day, concerning ceremonies, faith, and all else, new decrees which he sought to make as sacred and authoritative as the laws of Moses. Religion thus sank into a degrading superstition, while the true meaning and interpretation of the laws became corrupted. Furthermore, while the high priests were paving their way to the secular rule just after the restoration, they attempted to gain popular favour by assenting to every de-mand; approving whatever the people did, however impious, and accommodating Scripture to the very depraved current morals. Malachi bears witness to this in no measured terms: he chides the priests of his time as despisers of the name of God, and then goes on with his invective as follows (Mal ii:7, 8): "For the priest's lips should keep knowledge, and they should seek the law at his mouth: for he is the messenger of the Lord of hosts. But ye are departed out of the way; ye have caused many to stumble at the law, ye have corrupted the covenant of Levi, saith the Lord of hosts." He further accuses them of interpreting the laws according to their own pleasure, and paying no respect to God but only to persons. It is certain that the high priests were never so cautious in their conduct as to escape the remark of the more shrewd among the people, for the latter were at length emboldened to assert that no laws ought to be kept save those that were written, and that the decrees which the Pharisees (consisting, as Josephus says in his " Amtiquities," chiefly, of the common people), were deceived into calling the traditions of the fathers, should not be observed at all. However this may be, we can in nowise doubt that flattery of the high priest, the corruption of religion and the laws, and the enormous increase of the extent of the last-named, gave very great and frequent occasion for disputes and altercations impossible to allay. When men begin to quarrel with all the ardour of superstition, and the magistracy to back up one side or the other, they can never come to a compromise, but are bound to split into sects.

II.   It is worthy of remark that the prophets, who were in a private station of life, rather irritated than reformed mankind by their freedom of warning, rebuke, and censure; whereas the kings, by their reproofs and punishments, could always produce an effect. The prophets were often intolerable even to pious kings, on account of the authority they assumed for judging whether an action was right or wrong, or for reproving the kings themselves if they dared to transact any business, whether public or private, without prophetic sanction. King Asa who, according to the testimony of Scripture, reigned piously, put the prophet Hanani into a prison-house because he had ventured freely to chide and reprove him for entering into a covenant with the king of Armenia.

Other examples might be cited, tending to prove that religion gained more harm than good by such freedom, not to speak of the further consequence, that if the prophets had retained their rights, great civil wars would have resulted.

III.   It is remarkable that during all the period, during which the people held the reins of power, there was only one civil war, and that one was completely extinguished, the conquerors taking such pity on the conquered, that they endeavoured in every way to reinstate them in their former dignity and power. But after that the people, little accustomed to kings, changed its first form of government into a monarchy, civil war raged almost continuously; and battles were so fierce as to exceed all others recorded; in one engagement (taxing our faith to the utmost) five hundred thousand Israelites were slaughtered by the men of Judah, and in another the Israelites slew great numbers of the men of Judah (the figures are not given in Scripture), almost razed to the ground the walls of Jerusalem, and sacked the Temple in their unbridled fury. At length, laden with the spoils of their brethren, satiated with blood, they took hostages, and leaving the king in his well-nigh devastated kingdom, laid down their arms, relying on the weakness rather than the good faith of their foes. A few years after, the men of Judah, with recruited strength, again took the field, but were a second time beaten by the Israelites, and slain to the number of a hundred and twenty thousand, two hundred thousand of their wives and children were led into captivity, and a great booty again seized. Worn out with these and similar battles set forth at length in their histories, the Jews at length fell a prey to their enemies.

Furthermore, if we reckon up the times during which peace prevailed under each form of government, we shall find a great discrepancy. Before the monarchy forty years and more often passed, and once eighty years (an almost unparalleled period), without any war, foreign or civil. After the kings acquired sovereign power, the fighting was no longer for peace and liberty, but for glory; accordingly we find that they all, with the exception of Solomon (whose virtue and wisdom would be better displayed in peace than in war) waged war, and finally a fatal desire for power gained ground, which, in many cases, made the path to the throne a bloody one.

Lastly, the laws, during the rule of the people, remained uncorrupted and were studiously observed. Before the monarchy there were very, few prophets to admonish the people, but after the establishment of kings there were a great number at the same time. Obadiah saved a hundred from death and hid them away, lest they should be slain with the rest. The people, so far as we can see, were never deceived by false prophets till after the power had been vested in kings, whose creatures many of the prophets were. Again, the people, whose heart was generally proud or humble according to its circumstances, easily corrected it-self under misfortune, turned again to God, restored His laws, and so freed itself from all peril; but the kings, whose hearts were always equally puffed up, and who could not be corrected without humiliation, clung pertinaciously to their vices, even till the last overthrow of the city.

We may now clearly see from what I have said:-

I.   How hurtful to religion and the state is the concession to ministers of religion of any power of issuing decrees or transacting the business of government: how, on the contrary, far greater stability is afforded, if the said ministers are only allowed to give answers to questions duly put to them, and are, as a rule, obliged to preach and practise the received and accepted doctrines.

II.   How dangerous it is to refer to Divine right matters merely speculative and subject or liable to dispute. The most tyrannical governments are those which make crimes of opinions, for everyone has an inalienable right over his thoughts—nay, such a state of things leads to the rule of popular passion.

Pontius Pilate made concession to the passion of the Pharisees in consenting to the crucifixion of Christ, whom he knew to be innocent. Again, the Pharisees, in order to shake the position of men richer than themselves, began to set on foot questions of religion, and accused the Sadducees of impiety, and, following their example, the vilest—hypocrites, stirred, as they pretended, by the same holy wrath which they called zeal for the Lord, persecuted men whose unblemished character and distinguished virtue had excited the popular hatred, publicly denounced their opinions, and inflamed the fierce passions of the people against them.

This wanton licence being cloaked with the specious garb of religion could not easily be repressed, especially when the sovereign authorities introduced a sect of which they, were not the head; they were then regarded not as interpreters of Divine right, but as sectarians—that is, as persons recognizing the right of Divine interpretation assumed by the leaders of the sect. The authority of the magistrates thus became of little account in such matters in comparison with the authority of sectarian leaders before whose interpretations kings were obliged to bow.

To avoid such evils in a state, there is no safer way, than to make piety and religion to consist in acts only—that is, in the practice of justice and charity, leaving everyone's judgment in other respects free. But I will speak of this more at length presently.

III.   We see how necessary it is, both in the interests of the state and in the interests of religion, to confer on the sovereign power the right of deciding what is lawful or the reverse. If this right of judging actions could not be given to the very prophets of God without great injury, to the state and religion, how much less should it be entrusted to those who can neither foretell the future nor work miracles! But this again I will treat of more fully hereafter.

IV.   Lastly,, we see how disastrous it is for a people unaccustomed to kings, and possessing a complete code of laws, to set up a monarchy. Neither can the subjects brook such a sway, nor the royal authority submit to laws and popular rights set up by anyone inferior to itself. Still less can a king be expected to defend such laws, for they were not framed to support his dominion, but the dominion of the people, or some council which formerly ruled, so that in guarding the popular rights the king would seem to be a slave rather than a master. The representative of a new monarchy will employ all his zeal in attempting to frame new laws, so as to wrest the rights of dominion to his own use, and to reduce the people till they find it easier to increase than to curtail the royal prerogative. I must not, however, omit to state that it is no less dangerous to remove a monarch, though he is on all hands admitted to be a tyrant. For his people are accustomed to royal authority and will obey no other, despising and mocking at any less august control.

It is therefore necessary, as the prophets discovered of old, if one king be removed, that he should be replaced by another, who will be a tyrant from necessity rather than choice. For how will he be able to endure the sight of the hands of the citizens reeking with royal blood, and to rejoice in their regicide as a glorious exploit? Was not the deed perpetrated as an example and warning for himself?

If he really wishes to be king, and not to acknowledge the people as the judge of kings and the master of himself, or to wield a precarious sway, he must avenge the death of his predecessor, making an example for his own sake, lest the people should venture to repeat a similar crime. He will not, however, be able easily to avenge the death of the tyrant by the slaughter of citizens unless he defends the cause of tyranny and approves the deeds of his predecessor, thus following in his footsteps.

Hence it comes to pass that peoples have often changed their tyrants, but never removed them or changed the monarchical form of government into any other.

The English people furnish us with a terrible example of this fact. They sought how to depose their monarch under the forms of law, but when he had been removed, they were utterly unable to change the form of government, and after much bloodshed only brought it about, that a new monarch should be hailed under a different name (as though it had been a mere question of names); this new monarch could only consolidate his power by completely destroying the royal stock, putting to death the king's friends, real or supposed, and disturbing with war the peace which might encourage discontent, in order that the populace might be engrossed with novelties and divert its mind from brooding over the slaughter of the king. At last, however, the people reflected that it had accomplished nothing for the good of the country beyond violating the rights of the lawful king and changing everything for the worse. It therefore decided to retrace its steps as soon as possible, and never rested till it had seen a complete restoration of the original state of affairs.

It may perhaps be objected that the Roman people was easily able to remove its tyrants, but I gather from its history a strong confirmation of my contention. Though the Roman people was much more than ordinarily capable of removing their tyrants and changing their form of government, inasmuch as it held in its own hands the power of electing its king and his successor, said being composed of rebels and criminals had not long been used to the royal yoke (out of its six kings it had put to death three), nevertheless it could accomplish nothing beyond electing several tyrants in place of one, who kept it groaning under a continual state of war, both foreign and civil, till at last it changed its government again to a form differing from monarchy, as in England, only in name.

As for the United States of the Netherlands, they have never, as we know, had a king, but only counts, who never attained the full rights of dominion. The States of the Netherlands evidently acted as principals in the settlement made by them at the time of the Earl of Leicester's mission: they always reserved for themselves the authority to keep the counts up to their duties, and the power to preserve this authority and the liberty of the citizens. They had ample means of vindicating their rights if their rulers should prove tyrannical, and could impose such restraints that nothing could be done without their consent and approval.

Thus the rights of sovereign power have always been vested in the States, though the last count endeavoured to usurp them. It is therefore little likely that the States should give them up, especially as they have just restored their original dominion, lately almost lost.

These examples, then, confirm us in our belief, that every dominion should retain its original form, and, indeed, cannot change it without danger of the utter ruin of the whole state. Such are the points I have here thought worthy of remark.

CHAPTER XIX

It is Shown That the Right Over Matters Spiritual Lies Wholly With the Sovereign, And That the Outward Forms of Religion Should be in Accordance With Public Peace, If We Would Obey God Aright.

WHEN I said that the possessors of sovereign power have rights over everything, and that all rights are dependent on their decree, I did not merely mean temporal rights, but also spiritual rights; of the latter, no less than the former, they ought to be the interpreters and the champions. I wish to draw special attention to this point, and to discuss it fully in this chapter, because many persons deny that the right of deciding religious questions belongs to the sovereign power, and refuse to acknowledge it as the interpreter of Divine right. They accordingly assume full licence to accuse and arraign it, nay, even to excommunicate it from the Church, as Ambrosius treated the Emperor Theodosius in old time. However, I will show later on in this chapter that they take this means of dividing the government, and paving the way to their own ascendancy. I wish, however, first to point out that religion acquires its force as law solely from the decrees of the sovereign. God has no special kingdom among men except in so far as He reigns through temporal rulers. Moreover, the rites of religion and the outward observances of piety should be in accordance with the public peace and well-being, and should therefore be determined by the sovereign power alone. I speak here only of the outward observances of piety and the external rites of religion, not of piety, itself, nor of the inward worship of God, nor the means by which the mind is inwardly led to do homage to God in singleness of heart.

Inward worship of God and piety in itself are within the sphere of everyone's private rights, and cannot be alienated (as I showed at the end of Chapter VII.). What I here mean by the kingdom of God is, I think, sufficiently clear from what has been said in Chapter XIV. I there showed that a man best fulfils Gods law who worships Him, according to His command, through acts of justice and charity; it follows, therefore, that wherever justice and charity have the force of law and ordinance, there is God's kingdom.

I recognize no difference between the cases where God teaches and commands the practice of justice and charity through our natural faculties, and those where He makes special revelations; nor is the form of the revelation of importance so long as such practice is revealed and becomes a sovereign and supreme law to men. If, therefore, I show that justice and charity can only acquire the force of right and law through the rights of rulers, I shall be able readily to arrive at the conclusion (seeing that the rights of rulers are in the possession of the sovereign), that religion can only acquire the force of right by means of those who have the right to command, and that God only rules among men through the instrumentality of earthly potentates. It follows from what has been said, that the practice of justice and charity only acquires the force of law through the rights of the sovereign authority; for we showed in Chapter XVI. that in the state of nature reason has no more rights than desire, but that men living either by the laws of the former or the laws of the latter, possess rights coextensive with their powers.

For this reason we could not conceive sin to exist in the state of nature, nor imagine God as a judge punishing man's transgressions; but we supposed all things to happen according to the general laws of universal nature, there being no difference between pious and impious, between him that was pure (as Solomon says) and him that was impure, because there was no possibility either of justice or charity.

In order that the true doctrines of reason, that is (as we showed in Chapter IV.), the true Divine doctrines might obtain absolutely the force of law and right, it was necessary that each individual should cede his natural right, and transfer it either to society as a whole, or to a certain body of men, or to one man. Then, and not till then, does it first dawn upon us what is justice and what is injustice, what is equity and what is iniquity.

Justice, therefore, and absolutely all the precepts of reason, including love towards one's neighbour, receive the force of laws and ordinances solely through the rights of dominion, that is (as we showed in the same chapter) solely on the decree of those who possess the right to rule. Inasmuch as the kingdom of God consists entirely in rights applied to justice and charity or to true religion, it follows that (as we asserted) the kingdom of God can only exist among men through the means of the sovereign powers; nor does it make any difference whether religion be apprehended by our natural faculties or by revelation: the argument is sound in both cases, inasmuch as religion is one and the same, and is equally revealed by God, whatever be the manner in which it becomes known to men.

Thus, in order that the religion revealed by the prophets might have the force of law among the Jews, it was necessary that every man of them should yield up his natural right, and that all should, with one accord, agree that they would only obey such commands as God should reveal to them through the prophets. Just as we have shown to take place in a democracy, where men with one consent agree to live according to the dictates of reason. Although the Hebrews furthermore transferred their right to God, they were able to do so rather in theory than in practice, for, as a matter of fact (as we pointed out above) they absolutely retained the right of dominion till they transferred it to Moses, who in his turn became absolute king, so that it was only through him that God reigned over the Hebrews. For this reason (namely, that religion only acquires the force of law by means of the sovereign power) Moses was not able to punish those who, before the covenant, and consequently while still in possession of their rights, violated the Sabbath (Exod. xvi:27), but was able to do so after the covenant (Numb. xv:36), because everyone had then yielded up his natural rights, and the ordinance of the Sabbath had received the force of law.

Lastly, for the same reason, after the destruction of the Hebrew dominion, revealed religion ceased to have the force of law; for we cannot doubt that as soon as the Jews transferred their right to the king of Babylon, the kingdom of God and the Divine right forthwith ceased. For the covenant wherewith they promised to obey all the utterances of God was abrogated; God's kingdom, which was based thereupon, also ceased. The Hebrews could no longer abide thereby, inasmuch as their rights no longer belonged to them but to the king of Babylon, whom (as we showed in Chapter xvi.) they were bound to obey in all things. Jeremiah (chap. xxix:7) expressly admonishes them of this fact: "And seek the peace of the city, whither I have caused you to be carried away captives, and pray unto the Lord for it; for in the peace thereof shall ye have peace." Now, they could not seek the peace of the City as having a share in its government, but only as slaves, being, as they were, captives; by obedience in all things, with a view to avoiding seditions, and by observing all the laws of the country, however different from their own. It is thus abundantly evident that religion among the Hebrews only acquired the form of law through the right of the sovereign rule; when that rule was destroyed, it could no longer be received as the law of a particular kingdom, but only as the universal precept of reason. I say of reason, for the universal religion had not yet become known by revelation. We may therefore draw the general conclusion that religion, whether revealed through our natural faculties or through prophets, receives the force of a command solely through the decrees of the holders of sovereign power; and, further, that God has no special kingdom among men, except in so far as He reigns through earthly potentates.

We may now see in a clearer light what was stated in Chapter IV., namely, that all the decrees of God involve eternal truth and necessity, so that we cannot conceive God as a prince or legislator giving laws to mankind. For this reason the Divine precepts, whether revealed through our natural faculties, or through prophets, do not receive immediately from God the force of a command, but only from those, or through the mediation of those, who possess the right of ruling and legislating. It is only through these latter means that God rules among men, and directs human affairs with justice and equity.

This conclusion is supported by experience, for we find traces of Divine justice only in places where just men bear sway; elsewhere the same lot (to repeat, again Solomon's words) befalls the just and the unjust, the pure and the impure: a state of things which causes Divine Providence to be doubted by many who think that God immediately reigns among men, and directs all nature for their benefit.

As, then, both reason and experience tell us that the Divine right is entirely dependent on the decrees of secular rulers, it follows that secular rulers are its proper interpreters. How this is so we shall now see, for it is time to show that the outward observances of religion, and all the external practices of piety should be brought into accordance with the public peace and well-being if we would obey God rightly. When this has been shown we shall easily understand how the sovereign rulers are the proper interpreters of religion and piety.

It is certain that duties towards one's country are the highest that man can fulfil; for, if government be taken away, no good thing can last, all falls into dispute, anger and anarchy reign unchecked amid universal fear. Consequently there can be no duty towards our neighbour which would not become an offence if it involved injury to the whole state, nor can there be any offence against our duty towards our neighbour, or anything but loyalty in what we do for the sake of preserving the state. For instance: it is in the abstract my duty when my neighbour quarrels with me and wishes to take my cloak, to give him my coat also; but if it be thought that such conduct is hurtful to the maintenance of the state, I ought to bring him to trial, even at the risk of his being condemned to death.

For this reason Manlius Torquatus is held up to honour, inasmuch as the public welfare outweighed with him his duty towards his children. This being so, it follows that the public welfare is the sovereign law to which all others, Divine and human, should be made to conform. Now, it is the function of the sovereign only to decide what is necessary for the public welfare and the safety of the state, and to give orders accordingly; therefore it is also the function of the sovereign only to decide the limits of our duty towards our neighbour—in other words, to determine how we should obey God. We can now clearly understand how the sovereign is the interpreter of religion, and further, that no one can obey God rightly, if the practices of his piety do not conform to the public welfare; or, consequently, if he does not implicitly obey all the commands of the sovereign. For as by God's command we are bound to do our duty to all men without exception, and to do no man an injury, we are also bound not to help one man at another's loss, still less at a loss to the whole state. Now, no private citizen can know what is good for the state, except he learn it through the sovereign power, who alone has the right to transact public business: therefore no one can rightly practise piety or obedience to God, unless he obey the sovereign power's commands in all things. This proposition is confirmed by the facts of experience. For if the sovereign adjudge a man to be worthy of death or an enemy, whether he be a citizen or a foreigner, a private individual or a separate ruler, no subject is allowed to give him assistance. So also though the Jews were bidden to love their fellow-citizens as themselves (Levit. xix:17, 18), they were nevertheless bound, if a man offended against the law, to point him out to the judge (Levit. v:1, and Deut. xiii:8, 9), and, if he should be condemned to death, to slay him (Deut. xvii:7).

Further, in order that the Hebrews might preserve the liberty they had gained, and might retain absolute sway over the territory they had conquered, it was necessary, as we showed in Chapter xvii., that their religion should be adapted to their particular government, and that they should separate themselves from the rest of the nations: wherefore it was commanded to them, "Love thy neighbour and hate thine enemy" (Matt. v:43), but after they had lost their dominion and had gone into captivity in Babylon, Jeremiah bid them take thought for the safety of the state into which they had been led captive; and Christ when He saw that they would be spread over the whole world, told them to do their duty by all men without exception; all of which instances show that religion has always been made to conform to the public welfare. Perhaps someone will ask: By what right, then, did the disciples of Christ, being private citizens, preach a new religion? I answer that they did so by the right of the power which they had received from Christ against unclean spirits (see Matt. x:1). I have already stated in Chapter xvi. that all are bound to obey a tyrant, unless they have received from God through undoubted revelation a promise of aid against him; so let no one take example from the Apostles unless he too has the power of working miracles. The point is brought out more clearly by Christ's command to His disciples, "Fear not those who kill the body" (Matt. x:28). If this command were imposed on everyone, governments would be founded in vain, and Solomon's words (Prov. xxiv:21), "My son, fear God and the king," would be impious, which they certainly are not; we must therefore admit that the authority which Christ gave to His disciples was given to them only, and must not be taken as an example for others.

I do not pause to consider the arguments of those who wish to separate secular rights from spiritual rights, placing the former under the control of the sovereign, and the latter under the control of the universal Church; such pretensions are too frivolous to merit refutation. I cannot however, pass over in silence the fact that such persons are woefully deceived when they seek to support their seditious opinions (I ask pardon for the somewhat harsh epithet) by the example of the Jewish high priest, who, in ancient times, had the right of administering the sacred offices. Did not the high priests receive their right by the decree of Moses (who, as I have shown, retained the sole right to rule), and could they not by the same means be deprived of it? Moses himself chose not only Aaron, but also his son Eleazar, and his grandson Phineas, and bestowed on them the right of administering the office of high priest. This right was retained by the high priests afterwards, but none the less were they delegates of Moses—that is, of the sovereign power. Moses, as we have shown, left no successor to his dominion, but so distributed his prerogatives, that those who came after him seemed, as it were, regents who administer the government when a king is absent but not dead.

In the second commonwealth the high priests held their right absolutely, after they had obtained the rights of principality in addition. Wherefore the rights of the high priesthood always depended on the edict of the sovereign, and the high priests did not possess them till they became sovereigns also. Rights in matters spiritual always remained under the control of the kings absolutely (as I will show at the end of this chapter), except in the single particular that they were not allowed to administer in person the sacred duties in the Temple, inasmuch as they were not of the family of Aaron, and were therefore considered unclean, a reservation which would have no force in a Christian community.

We cannot, therefore, doubt that the daily sacred rites (whose performance does not require a particular genealogy but only a special mode of life, and from which the holders of sovereign power are not excluded as unclean) are under the sole control of the sovereign power; no one, save by the authority or concession of such sovereign, has the right or power of administering them, of choosing others to administer them, of defining or strengthening the foundations of the Church and her doctrines; of judging on questions of morality or acts of piety; of receiving anyone into the Church or excommunicating him therefrom, or, lastly, of providing for the poor.

These doctrines are proved to be not only true (as we have already pointed out), but also of primary necessity for the preservation of religion and the state. We all know what weight spiritual right and authority carries in the popular mind: how everyone hangs on the lips, as it were, of those who possess it. We may even say that those who wield such authority have the most complete sway over the popular mind.

Whosoever, therefore, wishes to take this right away from the sovereign power, is desirous of dividing the dominion; from such division, contentions, and strife will necessarily spring up, as they did of old between the Jewish kings and high priests, and will defy all attempts to allay them. Nay, further, he who strives to deprive the sovereign power of such authority, is aiming (as we have said), at gaining dominion for himself. What is left for the sovereign power to decide on, if this right be denied him? Certainly nothing concerning either war or peace, if he has to ask another man's opinion as to whether what he believes to be beneficial would be pious or impious. Everything would depend on the verdict of him who had the right of deciding and judging what was pious or impious, right or wrong.

When such a right was bestowed on the Pope of Rome absolutely, he gradually acquired complete control over the kings, till at last he himself mounted to the summits of dominion; however much monarchs, and especially the German emperors, strove to curtail his authority, were it only by a hairsbreadth, they effected nothing, but on the contrary by their very endeavours largely increased it. That which no monarch could accomplish with fire and sword, ecclesiastics could bring about with a stroke of the pen; whereby we may easily see the force and power at the command of the Church, and also how necessary it is for sovereigns to reserve such prerogatives for themselves.

If we reflect on what was said in the last chapter we shall see that such reservation conduced not a little to the increase of religion and piety; for we observed that the prophets themselves, though gifted with Divine efficacy, being merely private citizens, rather irritated than reformed the people by their freedom of warning, reproof, and denunciation, whereas the kings by warnings and punishments easily bent men

to their will. Furthermore, the kings themselves, not possessing the right in question absolutely, very often fell away
from religion and took with them nearly the whole people.
The same thing has often happened from the same cause in
Christian states.

Perhaps I shall be asked, "But if the holders of sovereign power choose to be wicked, who will be the rightful champion of
piety? Should the sovereigns still be its interpreters? "I meet
them with the counter-question, "But if ecclesiastics (who are
also human, and private citizens, and who ought to mind only
their own affairs), or if others whom it is proposed to entrust
with spiritual authority, choose to be wicked, should they still
be considered as piety's rightful interpreters?" It is quite certain that when sovereigns wish to follow their own pleasure,
whether they have control over spiritual matters or not, the
whole state, spiritual and secular, will go to ruin, and it will go
much faster if private citizens seditiously assume the champi-
onship of the Divine rights.

Thus we see that not only is nothing gained by denying such
rights to sovereigns, but on the contrary, great evil ensues.
For (as happened with the Jewish kings who did not possess
such rights absolutely) rulers are thus driven into wickedness,
and the injury and loss to the state become certain and inevi-
table, instead of uncertain and possible. Whether we look to
the abstract truth, or the security of states, or the increase of
piety, we are compelled to maintain that the Divine right, or
the right of control over spiritual matters, depends absolutely
on the decree of the sovereign, who is its legitimate interpreter
and champion. Therefore the true ministers of God's word are
those who teach piety to the people in obedience to the authority of the sovereign rulers by whose decree it has been brought
into conformity with the public welfare.

There remains for me to point out the cause for the frequent
disputes on the subject of these spiritual rights in Christian
states; whereas the Hebrews, so far as I know, never, had any
doubts about the matter. It seems monstrous that a question
so plain and vitally important should thus have remained

undecided, and that the secular rulers could never obtain the prerogative without controversy, nay, nor without great danger of sedition and injury to religion. If no cause for this state of things were forthcoming, I could easily persuade myself that all I have said in this chapter is mere theorizing, or akind of speculative reasoning which can never be of any practical use. However, when we reflect on the beginnings of Christianity the cause at once becomes manifest. The Christian religion was not taught at first by kings, but by private persons, who, against the wishes of those in power, whose subjects they, were, were for a long time accustomed to hold meetings in secret churches, to institute and perform sacred rites, and on their own authority to settle and decide on their affairs without regard to the state, When, after the lapse of many years, the religion was taken up by the authorities, the ecclesiastics were obliged to teach it to the emperors themselves as they had defined it: wherefore they easily gained recognition as its teachers and interpreters, and the church pastors were looked upon as vicars of God. The ecclesiastics took good care that the Christian kings should not assume their authority, by prohibiting marriage to the chief ministers of religion and to its highest interpreter. They furthermore elected their purpose by multiplying the dogmas of religion to such an extent and so blending them with philosophy that their chief interpreter was bound to be a skilled philosopher and theologian, and to have leisure for a host of idle speculations: conditions which could only be fulfilled by a private individual with much time on his hands.

Among the Hebrews things were very differently arranged: for their Church began at the same time as their dominion, and Moses, their absolute ruler, taught religion to the people, arranged their sacred rites, and chose their spiritual ministers. Thus the royal authority carried very great weight with the people, and the kings kept a firm hold on their spiritual prerogatives.

Although, after the death of Moses, no one held absolute sway, yet the power of deciding both in matters spiritual and matters temporal was in the hands of the secular chief, as I have already pointed out. Further, in order that it might be taught religion and piety, the people was bound to consult the supreme judge no less than the high priest (Deut. xvii:9, 11). Lastly, though the kings had not as much power as Moses, nearly the whole arrangement and choice of the sacred ministry depended on their decision. Thus David arranged the whole service of the Temple (see 1 Chron. xxviii:11, 12, &c.); from all the Levites he chose twenty-four thousand for the sacred psalms; six thousand of these formed the body from which were chosen the judges and proctors, four thousand were porters, and four thousand to play on instruments (see 1 Chron. xxiii:4, 5). He further divided them into companies (of whom he chose the chiefs), so that each in rotation, at the allotted time, might perform the sacred rites. The priests he also divided into as many companies; I will not go through the whole catalogue, but refer the reader to 2 Chron. viii:13, where it is stated, "Then Solomon offered burnt offerings to the Lord . . . . . after a certain rate every day, offering according to the commandments of Moses;" and in verse 14, "And he appointed, according to the order of David his father, the courses of the priests to their service . . . . . . for so had David the man of God commanded." Lastly, the historian bears witness in verse 15: "And they departed not from the commandment of the king unto the priests and Levites concerning any matter, or concerning the treasuries."

From these and other histories of the kings it is abundantly evident, that the whole practice of religion and the sacred ministry depended entirely on the commands of the king.

When I said above that the kings had not the same right as Moses to elect the high priest, to consult God without intermediaries, and to condemn the prophets who prophesied during their reign; I said so simply because the prophets could, in virtue of their mission, choose a new king and give absolution for regicide, not because they could call a king who offended against the law to judgment, or could rightly act against him.[8]

---

8   See Endnote 33.

Wherefore if there had been no prophets who, in virtue of a special revelation, could give absolution for regicide, the kings would have possessed absolute rights over all matters both spiritual and temporal. Consequently the rulers of modern times, who have no prophets and would not rightly be bound in any case to receive them (for they are not subject to Jewish law), have absolute possession of the spiritual prerogative, although they are not celibates, and they will always retain it, if they will refuse to allow religious dogmas to be unduly multiplied or confounded with philosophy.

CHAPTER XX

That in A Free State Every Man May Think What He Likes, and Say What He Thinks.

IF men's minds were as easily controlled as their tongues, every king would sit safely on his throne, and government by compulsion would cease; for every subject would shape his life according to the intentions of his rulers, and would esteem a thing true or false, good or evil, just or unjust, in obedience to their dictates. However, we have shown already (Chapter XVII.) that no man's mind can possibly lie wholly at the disposition of another, for no one can willingly transfer his natural right of free reason and judgment, or be compelled so to do. For this reason government which attempts to control minds is accounted tyrannical, and it is considered an abuse of sovereignty and a usurpation of the rights of subjects, to seek to prescribe what shall be accepted as true, or rejected as false, or what opinions should actuate men in their worship of God. All these questions fall within a man's natural right, which he cannot abdicate even with his own consent.

I admit that the judgment can be biassed in many ways, and to an almost incredible degree, so that while exempt from direct external control it may be so dependent on another man's words, that it may fitly be said to be ruled by him; but although this influence is carried to great lengths, it has never gone so far as to invalidate the statement, that every man's understanding is his own, and that brains are as diverse as palates.

Moses, not by fraud, but by Divine virtue, gained such a hold over the popular judgment that he was accounted superhuman, and believed to speak and act through the inspiration of the Deity; nevertheless, even he could not escape murmurs and evil interpretations. How much less then can other monarchs avoid them! Yet such unlimited power, if it exists at all, must belong to a monarch, and least of all to a democracy, where the whole or a great part of the people wield authority collectively. This is a fact which I think everyone can explain for himself.

However unlimited, therefore, the power of a sovereign may be, however implicitly it is trusted as the exponent of law and religion, it can never prevent men from forming judgments according to their intellect, or being influenced by any given emotion. It is true that it has the right to treat as enemies all men whose opinions do not, on all subjects, entirely coincide with its own; but we are not discussing its strict rights, but its proper course of action. I grant that it has the right to rule in the most violent manner, and to put citizens to death for very trivial causes, but no one supposes it can do this with the approval of sound judgment. Nay, inasmuch as such things cannot be done without extreme peril to itself, we may even deny that it has the absolute power to do them, or, consequently, the absolute right; for the rights of the sovereign are limited by his power.

Since, therefore, no one can abdicate his freedom of judgment and feeling; since every man is by indefeasible natural right the master of his own thoughts, it follows that men thinking in diverse and contradictory fashions, cannot, without disastrous results, be compelled to speak only according to the dictates of the supreme power. Not even the most experienced, to say nothing of the multitude, know how to keep silence. Men's common failing is to confide their plans to others, though there be need for secrecy, so that a government would be most harsh which deprived the individual of his freedom of saying and teaching what he thought; and would be moderate if such freedom were granted. Still we cannot deny that authority may be as much injured by words as by actions; hence, although the freedom we are discussing cannot be entirely denied to subjects, its unlimited concession would be most baneful; we must, therefore, now inquire, how far such freedom can and ought to be conceded without danger to the peace of the state, or the power of the rulers; and this, as I said at the beginning of Chapter xvi., is my principal object. It follows, plainly, from the explanation given above, of the foundations of a state, that the ultimate aim of government is not to rule, or restrain, by fear, nor to exact obedience, but contrariwise, to free every man from fear, that he may live in all possible security; in other words, to strengthen his natural right to exist and work—without injury to himself or others.

No, the object of government is not to change men from rational beings into beasts or puppets, but to enable them to develope their minds and bodies in security, and to employ their reason unshackled; neither showing hatred, anger, or deceit, nor watched with the eyes of jealousy and injustice. In fact, the true aim of government is liberty.

Now we have seen that in forming a state the power of making laws must either be vested in the body of the citizens, or in a portion of them, or in one man. For, although mens free judgments are very diverse, each one thinking that he alone knows everything, and although complete unanimity of feeling and speech is out of the question, it is impossible to preserve peace, unless individuals abdicate their right of acting entirely on their own judgment. Therefore, the individual justly cedes the right of free action, though not of free reason and judgment; no one can act against the authorities without danger to the state, though his feelings and judgment may be at variance therewith; he may even speak against them, provided that he does so from rational conviction, not from fraud, anger, or hatred, and provided that he does not attempt to introduce any change on his private authority.

For instance, supposing a man shows that a law is repugnant to sound reason, and should therefore be repealed; if he submits his opinion to the judgment of the authorities (who, alone, have the right of making and repealing laws), and meanwhile acts in nowise contrary to that law, he has deserved well of the state, and has behaved as a good citizen should; but if he accuses the authorities of injustice, and stirs up the people against them, or if he seditiously strives to abrogate the law without their consent, he is a mere agitator and rebel.

Thus we see how an individual may declare and teach what he believes, without injury to the authority of his rulers, or to the public peace; namely, by leaving in their hands the entire power of legislation as it affects action, and by doing nothing against their laws, though he be compelled often to act in contradiction to what he believes, and openly feels, to be best.

Such a course can be taken without detriment to justice and dutifulness, nay, it is the one which a just and dutiful man would adopt. We have shown that justice is dependent on the laws of the authorities, so that no one who contravenes their accepted decrees can be just, while the highest regard for duty, as we have pointed out in the preceding chapter, is exercised in maintaining public peace and tranquillity; these could not be preserved if every man were to live as he pleased; therefore it is no less than undutiful for a man to act contrary to his country's laws, for if the practice became universal the ruin of states would necessarily follow.

Hence, so long as a man acts in obedience to the laws of his rulers, he in nowise contravenes his reason, for in obedience to reason he transferred the right of controlling his actions from his own hands to theirs. This doctrine we can confirm from actual custom, for in a conference of great and small powers, schemes are seldom carried unanimously, yet all unite in carrying out what is decided on, whether they voted for or against. But I return to my proposition.

From the fundamental notions of a state, we have discovered how a man may exercise free judgment without detriment to the supreme power: from the same premises we can no less easily determine what opinions would be seditious. Evidently those which by their very nature nullify the compact by which the right of free action was ceded. For instance, a man who holds that the supreme power has no rights over him, or that promises ought not to be kept, or that everyone should live as he pleases, or other doctrines of this nature in direct opposition to the above-mentioned contract, is seditious, not so much from his actual opinions and judgment, as from the deeds which they involve; for he who maintains such theories abrogates the contract which tacitly, or openly, he made with his rulers. Other opinions which do not involve acts violating the contract, such as revenge, anger, and t he like, are not seditious, unless it be in some. corrupt state, where superstitious and ambitious persons, unable to endure men of learning, are so popular with the multitude that their word is more valued than the law.

However, I do not deny that there are some doctrines which, while they are apparently only concerned with abstract truths and falsehoods, are yet propounded and published with unworthy motives. This question we have discussed in Chapter xv., and shown that reason should nevertheless remain unshackled. If we hold to the principle that a man's loyalty to the state should be judged, like his loyalty to God, from his actions only—namely, from his charity towards his neighbours; we cannot doubt that the best government will allow freedom of philosophical speculation no less than of religious belief. I confess that from such freedom inconveniences may sometimes arise, but what question was ever settled so wisely that no abuses could possibly spring therefrom? He who seeks to regulate everything by law, is more likely to arouse vices than to reform them. It is best to grant what cannot be abolished, even though it be in itself harmful. How many evils spring from luxury, envy, avarice, drunkenness, and the like, yet these are tolerated—vices as they are—because they cannot be prevented by legal enactments. How much more then should free thought be granted, seeing that it is in itself a virtue and that it cannot be crushed! Besides, the evil results can easily be checked, as I will show, by the secular authorities, not to mention that such freedom is absolutely necessary for progress in science and the liberal arts: for no man follows such pursuits to advantage unless his judgment be entirely free and unhampered.

But let it be granted that freedom may be crushed, and men be so bound down, that they do not dare to utter a whisper, save at the bidding of their rulers; nevertheless this can never be carried to the pitch of making them think according to authority, so that the necessary consequences would be that men would daily be thinking one thing and saying another, to the corruption of good faith, that mainstay of government, and to the fostering of hateful flattery and perfidy, whence spring stratagems, and the corruption of every good art.

It is far from possible to impose uniformity of speech, for the more rulers strive to curtail freedom of speech, the more obstinately are they resisted; not indeed by the avaricious, the flatterers, and other numskulls, who think supreme salvation consists in filling their stomachs and gloating over their money-bags, but by those whom good education, sound morality, and virtue have rendered more free. Men, as generally constituted, are most prone to resent the branding as criminal of opinions which they believe to be true, and the proscription as wicked of that which inspires them with piety towards God and man; hence they are ready to forswear the laws and conspire against the authorities, thinking it not shameful but honourable to stir up seditions and perpetuate any sort of crime with this end in view. Such being the constitution of human nature, we see that laws directed against opinions affect the generous minded rather than the wicked, and are adapted less for coercing criminals than for irritating the upright; so that they cannot be maintained without great peril to the state.

Moreover, such laws are almost always useless, for those who hold that the opinions proscribed are sound, cannot possibly obey the law; whereas those who already reject them as false, accept the law as a kind of privilege, and make such boast of it, that authority is powerless to repeal it, even if such a course be subsequently desired.

To these considerations may be added what we said in Chapter XVIII. in treating of the history of the Hebrews. And, lastly, how many schisms have arisen in the Church from the attempt of the authorities to decide by law the intricacies of theological controversy! If men were not allured by the hope of getting the law and the authorities on their side, of triumphing over their adversaries in the sight of an applauding multitude, and of acquiring honourable distinctions, they would not strive so maliciously, nor would such fury sway their minds. This is taught not only by reason but by daily examples, for laws of this kind prescribing what every man shall believe and forbidding anyone to speak or write to the contrary, have often been passed, as sops or concessions to the anger of those who cannot tolerate men of enlightenment, and who, by such harsh and crooked enactments, can easily turn the devotion of the masses into fury and direct it against whom they will. How much better would it be to restrain popular anger and fury, instead of passing useless laws, which can only be broken by those who love virtue and the liberal arts, thus paring down the state till it is too small to harbour men of talent. What greater misfortune for a state can be conceived then that honourable men should be sent like criminals into exile, because they hold diverse opinions which they cannot disguise? What, I say, can be more hurtful than that men who have committed no crime or wickedness should, simply because they are enlightened, be treated as enemies and put to death, and that the scaffold, the terror of evil-doers, should become the arena where the highest examples of tolerance and virtue are displayed to the people with all the marks of ignominy that authority can devise?

He that knows himself to be upright does not fear the death of a criminal, and shrinks from no punishment; his mind is not wrung with remorse for any disgraceful deed: he holds that death in a good cause is no punishment, but an honour, and that death for freedom is glory.

What purpose then is served by the death of such men, what example in proclaimed? the cause for which they die is unknown to the idle and the foolish, hateful to the turbulent, loved by the upright. The only lesson we can draw from such scenes is to flatter the persecutor, or else to imitate the victim.

If formal assent is not to be esteemed above conviction, and if governments are to retain a firm hold of authority and not be compelled to yield to agitators, it is imperative that freedom of judgment should be granted, so that men may live together in harmony, however diverse, or even openly contradictory their opinions may be. We cannot doubt that such is the best system of government and open to the fewest objections, since it is the one most in harmony with human nature. In a democracy (the most natural form of government, as we have shown in Chapter xvi.) everyone submits to the control of authority over his actions, but not over his judgment and reason; that is, seeing that all cannot think alike, the voice of the majority has the force of law, subject to repeal if circumstances bring about a change of opinion. In proportion as the power of free judgment is withheld we depart from the natural condition of mankind, and consequently the government becomes more tyrannical.

In order to prove that from such freedom no inconvenience arises, which cannot easily be checked by the exercise of the sovereign power, and that men's actions can easily be kept in bounds, though their opinions be at open variance, it will be well to cite an example. Such an one is not very, far to seek. The city of Amsterdam reaps the fruit of this freedom in its own great prosperity and in the admiration of all other people. For in this most flourishing state, and most splendid city, men of every, nation and religion live together in the greatest harmony, and ask no questions before trusting their goods to a fellow-citizen, save whether he be rich or poor, and whether he generally acts honestly, or the reverse. His religion and sect is considered of no importance: for it has no effect before the judges in gaining or losing a cause, and there is no sect so despised that its followers, provided that they harm no one, pay every man his due, and live uprightly, are deprived of the protection of the magisterial authority.

On the other hand, when the religious controversy between Remonstrants and Counter-Remonstrants began to be taken up by politicians and the States, it grew into a schism, and abundantly showed that laws dealing with religion and seeking to settle its controversies are much more calculated to irritate than to reform, and that they give rise to extreme licence: further, it was seen that schisms do not originate in a love of truth, which is a source of courtesy and gentleness, but rather in an inordinate desire for supremacy, From all these considerations it is clearer than the sun at noonday, that the true schismatics are those who condemn other men's writings, and seditiously stir up the quarrelsome masses against their authors, rather than those authors themselves, who generally write only for the learned, and appeal solely to reason. In fact, the real disturbers of the peace are those who, in a free state, seek to curtail the liberty of judgment which they are unable to tyrannize over.

I have thus shown:-

I.   That it is impossible to deprive men of the liberty of saying what they think.

II. That such liberty can be conceded to every man without injury to the rights and authority of the sovereign power, and that every man may retain it without injury to such rights, provided that he does not presume upon it to the extent of introducing any new rights into the state, or act-ing in any way contrary, to the existing laws.

III. That every man may enjoy this liberty without detriment to the public peace, and that no inconveniences arise there-from which cannot easily be checked.

IV. That every man may enjoy it without injury to his allegiance.

V.   That laws dealing with speculative problems are entirely useless.

VI. Lastly, that not only may such liberty be granted without prejudice to the public peace, to loyalty, and to the rights of rulers, but that it is even necessary, for their preserva-tion. For when people try to take it away, and bring to trial, not only the acts which alone are capable of offend-ing, but also the opinions of mankind, they only succeed in surrounding their victims with an appearance of mar-tyrdom, and raise feelings of pity and revenge rather than of terror. Uprightness and good faith are thus corrupted, flatterers and traitors are encouraged, and sectarians triumph, inasmuch as concessions have been made to their animosity, and they have gained the state sanction for the doctrines of which they are the interpreters. Hence they arrogate to themselves the state authority and rights, and do not scruple to assert that they have been directly chosen by God, and that their laws are Divine, whereas the laws of the state are human, and should therefore yield obedience to the laws of God—in other words, to their own laws. Everyone must see that this is not a state of affairs conducive to public welfare. Wherefore, as we have shown in Chapter xviii., the safest way for a state is to lay down the rule that religion is comprised solely in the exercise of charity and justice, and that the rights of rulers in sacred, no less than in secular matters, should merely have to do with actions, but that every man should think what he likes and say what he thinks.

I have thus fulfilled the task I set myself in this treatise. It remains only to call attention to the fact that I have written nothing which I do not most willingly submit to the examination and approval of my country's rulers; and that I am willing to retract anything which they shall decide to be repugnant to the laws, or prejudicial to the public good. I know that I am a man, and as a man liable to error, but against error I have taken scrupulous care, and have striven to keep in entire accordance with the laws of my country, with loyalty, and with morality.

END OF PART IV

Author's Endnotes to the

Theologico-Political Treatise

CHAPTERS XVI TO XX

CHAPTER XVI

Endnote 26. "No one can honestly promise to forego the right which he has over all things." In the state of social life, where general right determines what is good or evil, stratagem is rightly distinguished as of two kinds, good and evil. But in the state of Nature, where every man is his own judge, possessing the absolute right to lay down laws for himself, to interpret them as he pleases, or to abrogate them if he thinks it convenient, it is not conceivable that stratagem should be evil.

Endnote 27. "Every member of it may, if he will, be free." Whatever be the social state a man finds; himself in, he may be free. For certainly a man is free, in so far as he is led by reason. Now reason (though Hobbes thinks otherwise) is always on the side of peace, which cannot be attained unless the general laws of the state be respected. Therefore the more he is free, the more constantly will he respect the laws of his country, and obey the commands of the sovereign power to which he is subject.

Endnote 28. "No one knows by nature that he owes any obedience to God." When Paul says that men have in themselves no refuge, he speaks as a man: for in the ninth chapter of the same epistle he expressly teaches that God has mercy on whom He will, and that men are without excuse, only because they are in God's power like clay in the hands of a potter, who out of the same lump makes vessels, some for honour and some for dishonour, not because they have been forewarned. As regards the Divine natural law whereof the chief commandment is, as we have said, to love God, I have called it a law in the same sense, as philosophers style laws those general rules of nature, according to which everything happens. For the love of God is not a state of obedience: it is a virtue which necessarily exists in a man who knows God rightly. Obedience has regard to the will of a ruler, not to necessity and truth. Now as we are ignorant of the nature of God's will, and on the other hand know that everything happens solely by God's power, we cannot, except through revelation, know whether God wishes in any way to be honoured as a sovereign.

Again; we have shown that the Divine rights appear to us in the light of rights or commands, only so long as we are ignorant of their cause: as soon as their cause is known, they cease to be rights, and we embrace them no longer as rights but as eternal truths; in other words, obedience passes into love of God, which emanates from true knowledge as necessarily as light emanates from the sun. Reason then leads us to love God, but cannot lead us to obey Him; for we cannot embrace the commands of God as Divine, while we are in ignorance of their cause, neither can we rationally conceive God as a sovereign laying down laws as a sovereign.

CHAPTER XVII

Endnote 29. "If men could lose their natural rights so as to be absolutely unable for the future to oppose the will of the sovereign" Two common soldiers undertook to change the Roman dominion, and did change it. (Tacitus, Hist. i:7.)

Endnote 30. See Numbers xi. 28. In this passage it is written that two men prophesied in the camp, and that Joshua wished to punish them. This he would not have done, if it had been lawful for anyone to deliver the Divine oracles to the people without the consent of Moses. But Moses thought good to pardon the two men, and rebuked Joshua for exhorting him to use his royal prerogative, at a time when he was so weary of reigning, that he preferred death to holding undivided sway (Numb. xi:14). For he made answer to Joshua, "Enviest thou for my sake? Would God that all the Lord's people were prophets, and that the Lord would put His spirit upon them." That is to say, would God that the right of taking counsel of God were general, and the power were in the hands of the people. Thus Joshua was not mistaken as to the right, but only as to the time for using it, for which he was rebuked by Moses, in the same way as Abishai was rebuked by David for counselling that Shimei, who had undoubtedly been guilty of treason, should be put to death. See 2 Sam. xix:22, 23.

Endnote 31. See Numbers xxvii:21. The translators of the Bible have rendered incorrectly verses 19 and 23 of this chapter. The passage does not mean that Moses gave precepts or advice to Joshua, but that he made or established him chief of the Hebrews. The phrase is very freguent in Scripture (see Exodus, xviii:23; 1 Sam. xiii:15; Joshua i:9; 1 Sam. xxv:80).

Endnote 32. "There was no judge over each of the captains save God." The Rabbis and some Christians equally foolish pretend that the Sanhedrin, called "the great" was instituted by Moses. As a matter of fact, Moses chose seventy colleagues to assist him in governing, because he was not able to bear alone the burden of the whole people; but he never passed any law for forming a college of seventy members; on the contrary he ordered every tribe to appoint for itself, in the cities which God had given it, judges to settle disputes according to the laws which he himself had laid down. In cases where the opinions of the judges differed as to the interpretation of these laws, Moses bade them take counsel of the High Priest (who was the chief interpreter of the law), or of the chief judge, to whom they were then subordinate (who had the right of consulting the High Priest), and to decide the dispute in accordance with the answer obtained. If any subordinate judge should assert, that he was not bound by the decision of the High Priest, received either directly or through the chief of his state, such an one was to be put to death (Deut. xvii:9) by the chief judge, whoever he might be, to whom he was a subordinate. This chief judge would either be Joshua, the supreme captain of the whole people, or one of the tribal chiefs who had been entrusted, after the division of the tribes, with the right of consulting the high priest concerning the affairs of his tribe, of deciding on peace or war, of fortifying towns, of appointing inferior judges, &c. Or, again, it might be the king, in whom all or some of the tribes had vested their rights.I could cite many instances in confirmation of what I here advance. I will confine myself to one, which appears to me the most important of all. When the Shilomitish prophet anointed Jeroboam king, he, in so doing, gave him the right of consulting the high priest, of appointing judges, &c. In fact he endowed him with all the rights over the ten tribes, which Rehoboam retained over the two tribes. Consequently Jeroboam could set up a supreme council in his court with as much right as Jehoshaphat could at Jerusalem (2 Chron. xix:8). For it is plain that neither Jeroboam, who was king by God's command, nor Jeroboam's subjects, were bound by the Law of Moses to accept the judgments of Rehoboam, who was not their king. Still less were they under the jurisdiction of the judge, whom Rehoboam had set up in Jerusalem as subordinate to himself. According, therefore, as the Hebrew dominion was divided, so was a supreme council setup in each division. Those who neglect the variations in the constitution of the Hebrew States, and confuse them all together in one, fall into numerous difficulties.

CHAPTER XIX

Endnote 33.　　I must here bespeak special attention for what was said in Chap. xvi. concerning rights.

End of Endnotes to PART IV

www.ingramcontent.com/pod-product-compliance
Lightning Source LLC
Chambersburg PA
CBHW021212020426

42331CB00003B/322